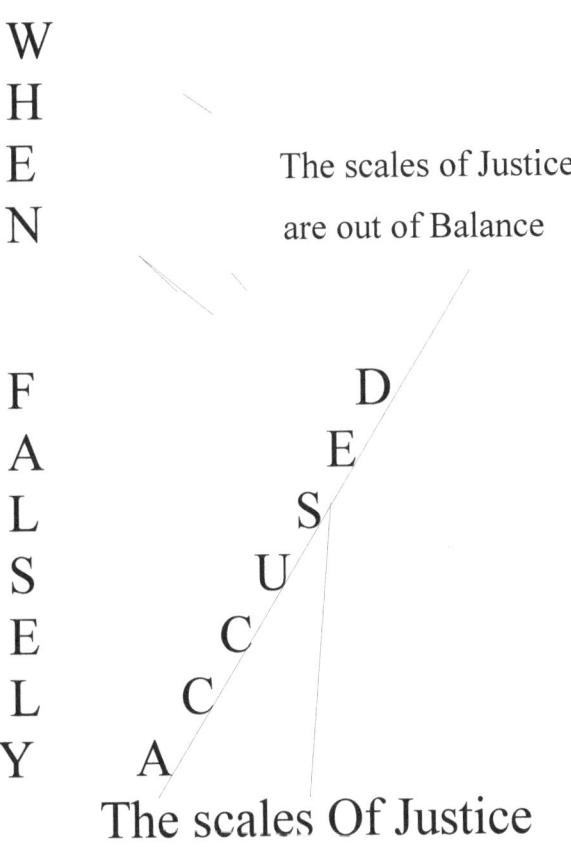

W
H
E   The scales of Justice
N   are out of Balance

F   D
A   E
L   S
S   U
E   C
L   C
Y   A

The scales Of Justice

When the gavel falls
A life has been changed

Joseph W. Kincade Jr

When Falsely Accused

This book is the opinion of the author and is noway to be construed as a rule of law.

All   quotes of scripture is from the NKJ

Joseph W. Kincade Jr

ISBN#:1467921246

Joseph W. Kincade Jr

Dedication

This book is dedicated to the people who has been falsely accused of a crime and found innocent, and being human enough to speak up in there behalf and are still struggling because of the conviction

Joseph W. Kincade Jr

CONTENTS

Joseph W. Kincade Jr

Joseph W. Kincade Jr

CHAPTER ONE

The Laws of this land are in place,to protect serve and to promote domestic tranquility sometime they are misplaced .Sometimes what you see is not the way it is

There was this queen ,who caught the kings eye and had made a demand on him for her favors, after the demand had been accepted she retired to her bedroom, she ordered a man killed over jealousy, for this man had great power , he was the kings second in command , and the king had promise her if you marry me I will give you as far as your eyes can see ,up to half of my kingdom,however material things was not in her consciousness, it was blood what she was after ,the man in charge under the king was a threat to her ,so he decided to go to her and plead for his life he entered her chambers and there she was dressed in the finest of silk ,the smell of incense was permeating the room ,the smell of aloe ,Myrah and Cinnamon was loud and inviting, he went to her bedside and fell upon his knees , and with a compassionate plea began to beg for his life At that moment the king walked in and all he could visualize, here , is a man trying to date my queen in my own house with me in it, Far from the truth, what you see is not always what it is.(Book of ESTHER- 7th Chapter 8th verse

Some times as humans we have a tendency to not accept apologizes, we instead ,try to visualize pain or misfortune for what we think is justifiable justice the allegations levied against us are true without evidence or manifestation of proof , the only thing that matters is, it was said, or what I saw , in turn which can be deceiving, what you see is not always what you get , an artist sees a mountain standing majestically with its snow top

Joseph W. Kincade Jr

peaks against the back drop of his canvas, while a skier sees a ski slope .If we can learn to adopt the theory that the only things that matters is the truth ,then I think that we will began to realize that lives has been destroyed because of gossip unintentionally ,no harm was foreseen ,however , it was done, we should be slow to speak so the bible say , what God is saying , check the plank in your eye be fore you look at the mote in mine,i am sure you will find for a better life to dwell upon if you stop looking at the way it was and adopt the truth of how it is.

An imaginative mind seems to disrupt every true thought that is perceive to its outcome. A adventurous imagination tends to, not be truthful without acknowledging it to a conscious fact,in other words what comes up comes out, without thought of consequences ,We have in our society a disruptive force call greed and self satisfaction, we tend to act upon dimension that accrue only to the avail, of its going to elevate me and belittle my subject, not knowing that, or knowing, that its going to destroy some part of me and that's to my satisfaction.

A policeman make an arrest knowing that he have no chance of holding his suspect but the thrill of showing his superiority over another human being is far to great of an opportunity to past up..

We tend to enjoy inserting additional knowledge of the subject that confronts us , by doing so it feed our ego and we receive some false kind of satisfaction to wit ,the putting down of our subject ,however we can never arrived at a truthful conclusion as to why , a lot of excuses be front us but never acknowledged. Why would one want to lock up or send to prison a person ,without being absolutely sure he has judge rightly,.You have to look at the power behind the decision or the motivation or the deliverer. Which is not always a proper thing to do considering the reputation you thought was upright and .Often

Joseph W. Kincade Jr

men of honor makes mistakes and they quickly rectify them, when they realize a harm had been committed .It wont correct the past however ,it will give some kind of solace to the victim,The time and
frustration that has been endured is not recoverable some kind of compensation is in order, but its not healing, The scares are there , the healing process is slow, time manages your recovery and god adjust your files..

For a wise man Pride has its limitations and adjust to the feeling of the soul,notwithstanding , one might summarize,for the contents of the soul is not contingency upon pride but however, emotions has it place, some small insignificant action that take place to address the outcome, will never take the place of true judgment, In the constitution it says that no law will be passed to abridge the articles that are written, The preamble has seven parts , it has been amended twenty seven times ,now, you might argue that and amendment is not a law , I wouldn't bet my scales of justice on it , anything that changes the course of another object that can effect the prior objects destiny is in affect a law.

To many times we misplace wise judgment to adhere to our own thought pattern, and we take some isolated incident and blow it out of proportion.

We have to endeavor to develop a system that's works for all people , rich or poor Protestant or Jew its just that simple.

People that are falsely accused are mostly devastated by this action while the accusations continue well up in ones life, the outsider stands and casually mentions well you know life goes on , yes it goes on, however, what about the pain of the victimize family not only do you ruin one life its a whole family involved, that's the consequences of bad judgment or emotional pride or the waggling of the tongue in a I think so position, not sure of what you ARE SAYING BECAUSE YOU DIDN'T

Joseph W. Kincade Jr

WITTNESS THE INCEDENT, you heard it from another source and the victim got accused without any consideration of the facts as long as I get my word in it doesn't matter he /she shouldn't have been caught up in the mess "Coal is coal as long as you don't polish it up and then it become a diamond, never to return to its original form ,as gossip, once its said , its out for to destroy anyone that listen , ninety five percent of gossip is a lie , and one hundred percent evil .

In this society we have a Murphy's law system that's say if any thing going to happen, it will , that's a hallucinatory statement that's not a fact that came out of the authors belief, which is the only thing he has control of , a statement made not in fact is a lie,although some would have you to believe otherwise , the black robes of justice sit in quite comfort knowing that there jobs are secure , so they judge according to there feeling simply because they have the power to change the law,not so you say , then why is there all the amendments.?

There is only one reason that is so they can have there way < Mr Thomas fought his way on accusations that wasn't true, an prevail he knew if he ever get in it was over , and he was compensated with a life time job that you have to die to lose it .

Where are the compensation for the victims in Mississippi and other renegade states a state that has no law for there disenfranchise victim is saying we are never wrong , we only make intentionally mistake ,The people that we arrest are a threat to society just by being born , never thinking that they have families that love them and need them consequences be hang we have to have conviction in this case , while the prosecution sit by and build evidence off theoretical hear say.

This man is guilty as charged , not knowing that the evidence presented might have been tainted or disturbed in some kind of

Joseph W. Kincade Jr

way and if he is black they never take time to find out "take him away he is guilty , I can look at him and tell",and life is just another day in the court room, with your eyes on   another conviction , there are some states that say if we are proven wrong we will take care of our victim and there families yet there are some that say we don't owe you a dime not even an apology .

Being in the wrong place at the wrong time has its draw backs but you have to prove beyond a shadow of a doubt that I wasn't suppose to be there , not what some young rookie cop looking for a collar said , or sometime wittiness looking for fame or maybe two dollars to get a bottle, cops do favors for criminals in return for favors ..

When The Gavel Falls

Joseph W. Kincade Jr

Chapter   Two

When the gavel falls a life has been taken, not literally, however taken, a man born into the world and the state law say we have a right to hold you as long as we see fit , and then let you go without explanation .

Its been recorded that ninety percent of these victim return to prison simply because the state took there former life from them and they have no where to go, there rights have to be restored to them those same rights shouldn't have been taken in the first place, the state say we are going to take your husband or son or daughter for a number of years now, you wait till he /or she gets out , we are not sure of what he done but we know he been doing something we just can't prove it .

That's the attitude of some, just to get a conviction , a judge tells a drug dealer that I am going to give you a year in the state penitentiary although I can't prove you are guilty I know you are a dealer I am going to show you how it feels to be locked up, no proof , just black and standing in the guilty box. You see it didn't matter if he were guilty are not he was in the drug crowd and he was lazy and black and automatically guilty, by associations, we pick your friends for you in this state , you don't have no say, not noting what the constitution says about the first amendment rights or that don't apply to you, the only part of the constitution that applies to you were when you were a slave , thirteenth and fourteenth amendment we will consider the provision there of .

Joseph W. Kincade Jr

Never let the outside world horrify your existent

Joseph W Kincade Jr

With liberty and justice for all , sounds like a foreign language to some, but the intention was well .or was it we will examine that .

With the economic woes passing on to a another President .The   intellectual Hippocrates of the former or present administration needs to be examined for corruption thereof.

We came from a balance budget to owing everybody in the world but yet our people suffer , there is no justice in taking care someone on distant soil when your own ground need plowing jobs are being shut down and the company's that moved overseas want to come back , because the workers of those foreign countries are demanding the same wages as American. Autoworker make cars at Thirty Dollars an hours to sell to a consumer that's making Six fifty an hour tell me I have gone crazy or I am asleep.

Mr Obama was Falsely Accused even before he took office its been said that he was linked to a terrorists that's get right back to choosing your friends for you.

A change has come to America , and needless to say," its about time" just maybe some of these people that's on death row will get a revue to ascertain if they are being tried for the crime they allegedly committed,There   should be a committee to over see this   there are far to many people behind bars   that are innocent   and want be compensated when they are released

Joseph W. Kincade Jr

with DNA testing it can be relatively simple, this should be taking in consideration when they are convicted.

Sitting in a Six By Ten Prison Cell isn't much fun when you no in your heart that you are innocent there are enough guilty people that's walking the street and some technicality got them off and they are laughing at the system knowing they have beat the system with their on laws . Honesty is against you in some cases .In the course of everyday life we sometime encounter problem that we think should end all problems. and then we read in the news that a guy has been released from prison that were not guilty ,after a fifteen year stretch,that's hard to believe In our society,we are the most productive people in the entire universe and yet we can't find a man innocent that's innocent,fifteen years the story reads and he were told to go home without any compensation or I am sorry , not to mention that he can appeal his case or reopen it to find the guilty party ,which they already had if not he would not be out ,how do he explain to his kids his absents ,the two year old is seventeen now and the ten year old is twenty five ,and it s hard to explain you didn't do what you were accused of ,it were a matter of being in the wrong place at the wrong time. DNA is a wonderful tool if you are innocent ,however, you had better be innocent, it works both ways to convict you or exonerate you,

Its been said that the man had been in a local bar and had a few to many ,knowing that he could get in a lot of trouble he decided to walk home a few blocks away ,which was a intelligent decision ,however it cost him fifteen years of his life

Walking home in happy mood sing those old blues songs it seems that everything was alright ,he came across this ally and heard this crying and sniffling so he decided to investigate ,for the shape he was in wrong move ,he stumbles along this ally holding on to the wall and the crying keep getting louder and louder as he approach the victim he knew something was wrong her clothes were torn of her parcel y and the her hair was in disarray,he knew that an attempt had been made to rape her ,he kept asking what happen ,but she kept yelling get away .he smelled of alcoholic and so did her assailant,who ever that was ,he was trying to help her and she thought otherwise,So he left ,and continued to walk home not knowing what were to take place the next day .

The next morning he decided to go and get his car,and he was approach by a police cruiser never noticing the passenger in the back she had fingered him as the suspect they went into the station to do a line up and sure enough she picked him as the assailant ,.far from the truth one can only imagine what question was asked to prove he was the suspect but we know they weren't pleasant ,when law enforcement decided to get a conviction ,some not all ,the truth is of little essence,they will manufacture evidence that's unbelievable,one guy said that policeman have an imagination that would shame Shakespeare ,it's so hard to tell what they are after anymore the truth or a collar,integrity is a word most of us can't spell let alone live by,and the attitude is what difference would it make anyway ,they are not going to believe me because they have an objective and it's not in your favor ,what you have to do is make sure you are well suited for the situation you are in,don't take for granted everything is AOK. and working good in your favor,take time to study the constitution its your secret weapon it were written so you would have a guideline to live by not for the lawyer to put you in jail,remember most of your officers don't know anymore about the law than you do,case in point most will arrest you without reading you your rights ,that's a walking point , most will search you not according to the fourth amendment.

And most will question you without the present of a lawyer. All

Joseph W. Kincade Jr

these little mistakes can mean freedom to you. Take advantage of all that,s there for you All these are violations of your civil rights ,but if you don't know them its like someone throwing a baseball at you and you are blind ,you have know way of knowing when to duck. Everyone facing a judge should have knowledge of there civil rights ,not necessarily the law, which was formed from the constitution ,but basic understanding of their civil rights .

When you sing my country tis of the sweet land of liberty basically what you are saying is I live in a country where I can express myself without repercussion knowing your rights is one of the basic civil rights issue that every American should know or have some knowledge of. The framers of this document where considered geniuses and the longevity of the document spells they are right it has been broken many time but not removed one of the articles have been amended twenty seven times and still standing thatch a fight that we as Americans consider worthy of a medal of honer. Thomas Jefferson conclude that a bill of rights was what every American citizen was entitled to against every government in the world they had to change the constitution, you pays him or the government pays, so whatever the situation he is getting paid to give you the best defense according to the constitution there is. The constitution will only endure as long as Americans will not permit its abuse, so far that has been the norm, the defendant in a case goes to jail for two reason maybe three he don't know his rights or he's guilty or maybe he was railroaded for a crime he didn't commit, it happens everyday and the later is not so unusual it happened to the defendant for-mention earlier the true assailant was found fifteen years later and eighteen hindered miles away, through DNA testing but that's fifteen years too late . There is no jobs for this guy, what he put on the resume, fifteen years in the state penitentiary, no I didn't learn a skill

Joseph W. Kincade Jr

while I was incarcerated, and the same o same o goes on every where he looks for a job, he is not eligible for unemployment because he has been in lock-down, working for no pay, or somewhere close to it, no food stamps, all his children is above dependent age, you talking about throwing a rat at the roach, so whats next,? You are not a criminal in the first place, the state say no compensation for the time spent in prison on a false charge. So you decide the best thing to do is find a lawyer and screen him very carefully no more taking your word for it. A lesson has been learned here and no more lies you have to prove to me now that what you say is true and what are your guidelines. How many of these case have you done, you had better find out where he stand because you are talking about suing the state for false imprisonment, and believe me you are about to create a lot of enemies, if you are able to find a lawyer. The stigma of you being in prison will stay with you the rest of your life the lawyers that you talk to will tell you that you don't have a case, the state law read no compensation for false imprisonment, but remind him that there is a federal law that overrides the state, there are nine seats up there that might think different and they might feel that you didn't get a trial, if you can get a copy of your case they will revue it for free, and render an opinion not a verdict then you are going to have to get a lawyer to reopen your case, but you have something to fight with. Don't let sleeping dogs lie too long they might get fleas, you have to act as fast as you can while your release is fresh and there are people around to testify of your case and character while incarcerated, even if you were not an ideal prisoner your situation warrants it. When we as a people live to indulge ourselves in only our miserable lives and discount people we have already lost the battle, if compassion is a by-word of your disdainful vocabulary then we have come to the conclusion, that I am all that matters, condemnation characterizing and

Joseph W. Kincade Jr

categorizing all seems to be the appropriate attitude for your situation. In other words when you walk in the court room they start sizing you up. There is one thing that you have at this point that is to keep silent and take a wait and see attitude or speak out and let them know that you are not for this kind of justice, any procedure that seems unreal ask your lawyer, and ask him if there is any kind of precedent set in this case and what are the guidelines, remember you are paying him or the government is paying, nevertheless he is getting paid its far to important to let another person make a decision as important that remember it is money that they are looking for, your freedom is second. We don't judge people however in the isles of justice you may have to size someone up just to get some kind of idea of where you stand a jury consultant does it all the time, they will hire the psychologist to sit behind a glass window and profile the individual that is to be a jury, they are trying to get a conviction any way they can don't too many people like losers. Lets get on another subject for a while, GOSSIPERS, just as categorically, as the man being falsely accused of something he didn't do as far as the listener is concerned its true, part maybe, but all the truth, never, its almost impossible for a person to carry something the way he got it, there is a add on factor juice it up, if you will, you must believe me attitude, why is it that they have to believe that if I add on to this little bit of gossip it will sound true and it want sound as if I am lying, they must know that I don't lie. And you just did., The hazards of gossip is so great that when someone approach you with some, he say she say conversation the question should be asked, how you know?, That's going to quieten things down for a while and then the argument will start, the conversation will go ,"you don't believe me," the answer should be ,"oh yes," but I just want to know how you know, and why people trust you with such information and you are telling me about it, do you not think that's a little

Joseph W. Kincade Jr

strange, of course you do, and I am also curious as to what your qualification are, to listen to such, have you ever thought of the devastation that one can cause by loose gossip, make sure that the information that you pass on is worthy of reproof if not its not worth talking about. In other words, you are starting something that has the potential to be very dangerous in someone life, saying things that you don't know if they are true or not has gotten people killed literally, There are so much wrong in all of us ,and no right in none of us,That it behoove all off us not to talk about the rest of us, case in point, read the book of Ester all the king saw was a man on his bed trying to seduce his woman, and what Haman was doing begging for his life, for she had order him behead, sad but true, how sometimes we make big mistakes and are so engrossed in popularity or prosperity that weren't the real issues. The king had made promises that he had to keep to the women he love, he had promised Ester that if she marry him he would give her anything she wanted up to half of his kingdom he had no idea that she was jealous of Haman position with the king, you see with all of his Witt and intelligence the king had made him second in command, but it were no match for Ester's beauty, she demanded his head on a charger the king didn't question her decision, that's what happen to most people that gossip they are never question about the factual contents of there conversation, gossip is the most misleading tool one could ever posses damaging and never meant to be harmful, however, it has cause wars, among nations and divorce and all other horrific things among individuals, we are to come and reason together, however, there is no reasonable explanation or platform that you can establish in this kind of situation, when the word was spoken the damage was done, retraction are rare in gossip, the gossiper don't want to be known as a lair or one who spreads false testimony, usually they are upstanding in the community

Joseph W. Kincade Jr

every one believe exactly what they say, they believe what someone told them. When you take a mans word for a truth you had better know where it is coming from, we are at a war at this writing, just because someone told someone a falsehood, statistic I will not quote but its devastating, families has been disrupted lives lost and children left to support themselves with no remorse-fulness I might add be careful what you talk about., I don't think I can put it more plainer than that. The big brass will tell you that freedom is expensive, I say that depends on who's buying we have a tendency in this country to get involved in everything from a dog fight to major insurgency, be hanged, and some guy wearing a star on his shoulder will send you the message, that it have arrived, the time to shine, and next it was greeting from the president and of to war you go,- we will tell why when you get back, if you get back, now you volunteer to be killed so they have no one to blame, and the answer will be to your loved ones, he ask for it. How gross, many of us went into the army because of Economic condition. Every   sex offender is required to register with local law enforcement upon his release and its not voluntary its mandatory, what about the guy that spent fifteen years of his life for something that he didn't do and it was proven in a court of law, do he register or not, his record is alive and well, next question do they destroy his record? Or do a judge close the file? Where it can't be open anymore. These question we are going to try and answer to the best of our ability.

Remember this is the authors opinion

We think that everything representing that case should be destroyed. This is a mans life we are talking about here and it should matter to the highest of degree, its unlikely that will happen its a lawyers world and we have to manipulate them like they are manipulating you. You see on his job resume he has a

Joseph W. Kincade Jr

non-productive period the only thing that's accountable for fifteen years is his prison record its noted that he was founded innocent of all charges. The definition of truth is, giving an accurate account of what happen or what has been seen heard or forced, however, getting someone to believe you is another matter, giving this assumption we must ask ourselves if the truth is at all possible, when information is passed between two or three hands, its inevitable the text or testimony will change and there you have the possibility of a lie. If we are ready to tell the truth and are willing to suffer the consequences for that action, even then can we tell the truth, we need to examine everything about what has happen and reexamine to make sure what we are about to give is what happen to the best of your knowledge, we have a tendency to restrain or change the truth when the pressure get too much for us to say exactly what happens or the fear of being found out. You may not have done anything, but fear takes over and that's the awful feeling, what comes to ones mind is they don't believe me, and then we start parting from the truth that's a bad move, stick with the truth its like love true, it want go away and it stays the same without change, that old saying that truth never changes that's true if its not manufactured, anything that's idealistic or compassionate have a life cycle that's operated thru emotion, emotions are untrustworthy they change with feelings and feelings are divided into two groups bad or good, in our governing body its been said and documented that all men are created equal, not so as to his situation, when question are being asked and opinion are being made that man whom has had a bad experience will get second justice! Oh!, they will try and play it down but a child can read where they are trying to go, and I am afraid that the finger will be pointed at the defendant for a long time. He himself want overcome but he will probably learn to live with it, in the back of his mind he will be thinking what kind of people

Joseph W. Kincade Jr

are this, most likely if a dollar is not attached to the thinker he want get very far its sad but we are our worse enemies if someone said it, bound to be true. Jesus said come let us reason together, that's a joke now days reasoning is what I say , and what you will listen to. Then its where do I go from here, long days of pounding the pavement and looking over my shoulder to see if anyone is looking at me and recognized who I am, the application for jobs are design for people who don't have a history, the question they ask are not design for ex-convicts even though you were proven to be the wrong man you a have been label as a ex-convict, so its in one place of employment or another, and you are getting the same answer every time, sorry, its a feeling that no man should have to experience, all kinds of thoughts go through your mind some not so pleasant, but remember you are a criminal whether you like or not them identity has been cast upon you without your consent, in your heart you know you are a law abiding citizen and that's what you are going to have to carry yourself as, bad thoughts will not be allowed wrong doing is conceived and when its acted upon its a crime and there we stand in the middle of controversy again, now going through your mind is if I had just given this a little more forethought, there is one thought that goes through the mind is the constitution its the oldest document in our system and yet it can be relied upon as our lifeline there was a time when it couldn't be, depend on who it was that it were being ask to defend. At the time these hollow words wrote they were not meant for everyone however all that change in later years, these are a few that it would do you justice to remember:

First amendment: congress shall make no law respecting an establishment of religion or prohibiting the free excise there of...

Second amendment: The right of the people to bear arms...

Third Amendment: No soldier shall be quartered in your house

Joseph W. Kincade Jr

without your consent...

Forth Amendment: the rights of the people to be safe and secure in there persons, houses papers against unreasonable searches and seizures

DNA is considered illegal search and seizure if consent not given by the suspect

Fifth Amendment: No person can be tried twice for the same offense.

Six Amendment: The accuse shall enjoy the right to a speedy trial.

Seventh Amendment: Where the value exceed twenty dollars the accuse shall preserve the right to be tried by jury and no fact tried by jury shall be reexamine by any other court in the United States of America.

Eight Amendment: Excessive fine shall not be imposed, nor excessive bail be set, nor cruel and unusual punishment be inflicted.

Take a little time and learn the constitution, the above is just a few, I was wondering what were the framers of the constitution, considering as unusual punishment it seems that a man locked up for a crime he didn't commit is unusual punishment. You can challenge any of the amendments to what avail I don't know. But before I sit and let them pass sentence I would pull out all the stops, everything that you are uncomfortable with, if you have a court appointed lawyer you are in big trouble, there problem wont be an appeal simply because you didn't have money for a lawyer in the first place, an appeal bond will cost you according to the crime that has been committed , the public offender could care less about your situation he is on salary there is no incentive to press on, you win some and lose some is

Joseph W. Kincade Jr

his attitude, but there are good ones out there that's concerned about your welfare if you are lucky enough to pull one, so what we do depend on the oldest document in our system, that's right. The constitution of the United States. It will always keep us and guide us if we respect it truthfully, which is getting harder and harder to do. Lawyers like to write there own laws and judges like to sit back as some above the rest, predominates and execute justice that's mostly not in line with constitution. The sex offender act will be challenged through our history because of the many faults that has showed up since its insurgency, the lawyers seeking the truth will have to first challenge the legal aspect of the law on this, compared to the constitution and the state, in which this trial is being carried out. You have the same right to go into the court house law library and research your case, to make sure you are getting a fair shake. The lawyer is always ready to claim for himself the merits of the badge for which he fights. It is extremely dangerous to pride oneself on any religious or moral issue that would not advance your case, what you are looking for is a win not a court of many colors, its a funny thing that when it comes to winning they will pull out all stops. Those same laws that they have been told not to use by the supreme court they will hold the book of rules up to the judge and show it like the judge don't know what to do, or don't know the law, its amazing how a law that's been viewed as unconstitutional can come in and out of focus as the preceding carry on without anyone noticing. How are you going to know how an individual is. First of all by his acts but by something else to-something that's only perceived by intuition, however glamorous or misleading that maybe. Soul judges soul by elective affinity, reaching through that's what perceive to be true and adjusting according both words and silence, looks and action, the accuracy in the judgment is in proportion to the moral character of the judge, the end of the climax would be,

Joseph W. Kincade Jr

justice served as universal law, not to deceive is its first desire, to be understood is second. It has been said that a man running from his past is a losing race, I say why let the government create one, and that will cut out the running. Emancipation from error is a condition from real knowledge, to admit you were wrong takes real courage and few that has it, pride has its strong hold, it does not see that pride is a condition of weakness and the ego bout the size of Texas, try to separate the thought from the thinker. Under the first amendment you cant petition the government for redress of grievances, congress shall make no law clause, took care of that and the forth amendment is in limbo on the search and seizure test if it works for you at your house, place of business what if you are driving a car drinking and they want to withdraw a sample of blood dose the Forth Amendment work the same as if it were at your house its being tested by the supreme court, it will be interesting to know what they will pass. False imprisonment is holding a person against his will for a unspecified amount of time it also say that the holder can be charged with a crime, !!WOW! Now that's very interesting because the state held this man without proper evidence to keep him and after DNA testing he was proven innocent, the charges against the state are, false imprisonment in the first degree, <question who serve the time for this crime and a crime has been committed, and the state is the defendant I wonder do they cry habas corpses, in order to find the guilty party. We have come to a state of mind in this country that whatever feel good, is good. America's obsession, with feeling good is causing us not to feel good, we arrest people and then go looking for a crime just to sit over a cup of coffee and brag about our collar. I am bouncing around a lot here but it is absolutely necessary for you to get the whole picture. People are lying in prison innocent as the day they were born and up until a few years ago they didn't have a chance now through DNA

Joseph W. Kincade Jr

testing its have become possible for them to be set free, one of the top lawyers in this country formed a company that petition the states for DNA if the inmate is willing to give a sample, all they have to do is request it or tell there lawyer to do so, if the DNA will clear them that's the way to go. The important thing is to not to lose hope, that's all you have at the present and it has grown thin I imagine, if you are a fighter you will win if not the consequences are devastating, don't let worry keep you from doing what you know to do, and if you don't know ask someone what do, its not a crime not to know but on the other hand not to ask. It's your life Charley brown

Take advantage of all the techniques available to you,DNA testing without the inmates consent is still up for grabs ,some congressmen think that they should submit to the invasion of your body without your consent ,however if you don't submit they will use the last evidence that they have to convict you ,it's been said that over half of the people that has consented were found to be innocent, i don;t understand the hast to convict a man or women when you are not sure of his innocent ,and you sit there and contemplate if you are going to go for the juggler vain or let him suffer slowly, It seems that their should be a redress of grievances .To absolutely be sure of what he is being charged with. The bible say come let us reason together,i guess the courts are excluded .,Of course that's normal, they take the word of GOD and put it every where its not suppose to be,even in the system of our government there are corruption,it always has been and always will be ,corrupt people will always create corrupt values.

Our society exalts vengeance ,We don't know if they are guilty ,so convict them anyway, by association ,-- my goodness what kind of people are we,90% of the worlds attorneys live in

Joseph W. Kincade Jr

the USA and we can't find a man innocent That's innocent, Sue for money that's our motto ,yet they can't compensate a man that's been locked up for a crime he didn't commit. Some states do ,however,most of them don,t I think that should be look into Mr. Obama Allows illegal aliens to live of our social rolls and can't give the working people of America a cost of living increase that' s American justice in a welfare basket .You go to work put your money into the system and someone else draws it out, That's not from your country and don't have a social security Card and probably not trying to get one,We have people in our system that literally can't afford there gas bill this year its so high ,they are having to choose between staying warm and eating And a man from somewhere across the world can sit in comfort and don't have to worry about even paying his bills that it take to survive .People are crossing our borders at an alarming rate ,you can't hire enough officers to keep them out it seems .Yet they are not even told to go home and they will stand up and say they are here legal and good old US of A is falsely accusing them of border running,and from these accusation will spin of a law suit of course compensation is in order you have degrade my integrity and cause me to look bad in front of my people .

It is foolish to think that fundamental change will come overnight,and its an illusion to think that it requires time so you put those two together and you are still at a cross road of condition moral issues and underlying appetites are so present that the only thing we see is, the end is near and not so devastating as it seems and then the ego takes over,and qualifies itself as the chief inspector knowing you are thinking ,I am innocent ,but why is it no one is listening ,Know one told you they were going to listen to you , the word was they are going to convict you, getting you off the streets is important while they ascertain your guilt, you even try to separate the thought from

Joseph W. Kincade Jr

the thinker at a huge failure ! You know what the heck, I won't be in here long ,so you thought .

Defined constitutional rights and a judicial system committed to protecting those rights provide Americans with the tools by which to defend themselves. Legal proceeding can be expensive,and they seems endless especially when decision are appealed . Falsely Accusing, been going on since Abraham Lincoln,Fred Korematsu , whose conviction for not appearing at a dentition center , had been upheld by the Supreme Court in 1944,was vindicated only in 1983,for many people that's injustice itself and then the long wait for a decision would provoke profound bitterness,that Mr Korematsu would say he was sent to jail as a criminal though innocent,I love this country and belong here , That's a testimony to the man , not to the United States .

The great importance which the framers of the constitution attached the privileges of the writ of habeas corpus to protect the liberty of the citizen,is provide by the fact that its suspension ,except in case of invasion is first on the list of prohibited power. The same holds true for the first Amendment Protection of Freedom of Speech,and you could go on and on about laws that was written to protect the people and one man could call the shot yet congress wrote the comparatively with the constitution,case in point ,the declaration   of war are supposed to be declared by congress however we have had at least three and congress never declared one, that power was passed on to the president so how can they hold him responsible ,so the truth is, he has been falsely appointed a duty that he is not responsible for,I bet they would argue that,on the grounds that he is the commander in chief In realty the congress of today is just the overseer of the presidents war to make sure he don't call the wrong shots without the responsibility of declaring war. The

Joseph W. Kincade Jr

Vietnam war and it sweeping operation was never declared nor was Iraq we like to go around falsely accusing people of doing something and then dare them to stand up for themselves,Just think one man can say what you can an can;'t do, that would cause thousand of lives to be destroyed that's! Awesome in any ones book ,of course,we are to busy condemning each other we can't see the real problem. If we observe ourselves in our action then we will see the real problem which is our thoughts and ego that has taken the place of good old common sense,If its going to put my name on a marque ,then it's got to be right. Thoughts of destruction never parallel with honest prosperity. They won't sit in the same run ,its a tug of war, Your thoughts arrive from your memory,be it good or bad .There is only one person that has a single minded thought of good and his name is GOD,for he said in the King James Version of the bible that my ways are not your ways and ,my thoughts are not your thoughts that I have of you yet we base all our laws on a document that was written according to the bible teaching and we can't have prayer in school, train a child in the way he must go ,and it will never depart from him ,sounds like a foreign language we have added so many amendments to our lives that we are running out of space ,capture the moment the heck with consequences we will worry about them later .You know we are all opinionated so why does yours have to be always wrong, an opinion is not the truth so why do lawyer right them as law ,?and you are judge by some of them they are quick to say it was the courts opinion in 1924 well was it the courts opinion that a man get convicted on circumstantial evidence and spend fifteen years in prison,for a crime he did not commit,you see opinions are dangerous coming out of the wrong mouth,that flag in the center of your head is an awesome tool it has no brain some time it speak to be heard not realizing the damage its causing,We divide and classify the world and then compare ourselves to it,in other words we built this castle and you have no right to inspect it .

The court was slow to uphold the rights of blacks ,for example the congress was going to pass a law that would   allow the railroad to initiate separate cars for,blacks   only one justice dissented he remarked that the separate but equal law would stimulate aggression,and so it did ,during that time the court wrote a law in its narrowest sense allowing it to pass with out much scrutiny,falsely accusing the blacks of being inferior to the whites or any other race that come along ,they name you a race by the color of your skin, forgetting there were and still is Black Indians,on a legal form it will either be Black or Indian. Who will correct that,?

  Today many school districts are still not fully integrated thou the law was struck down over sixty years ago   the thirteenth an fourteenth amendments guarantee equal rights under the law, don't you bet on it, If you believe in something you should be your best investigator get at the truth and stand by it ,bad times and trouble will follow but many men has died to see that the Constitution Of the United States Works , if not upheld in its present form all would have died for naught .We the people ,in order to form a more perfect union,!!What !,now we are saying that the union is perfect and we are going to make it more perfect Accusing the union of being perfect is like saying I can swim the Atlantic in one stroke   .Our fore-fathers had no intention of writing a document that were not viable and self serving The appointments are one of the most respected in the world the power that it carries is awesome ,you can literally change nations ,including this one direction with the stroke of a pen,What we are seeking is self-continuity ,to place in motion the immorality of our being ,we sometime forget that there are an ending and a beginning and anything in between is vanity it dose not matter if you make a law that will surpass all other laws

Joseph W. Kincade Jr

it will soon come around to being your turn. .

Article three- section 1 The judicial power shall be vested in one Supreme Court ,That's power, what ever I say that's it ,end of story,To whom were they addressing you can't go any father than the Supreme Court,Congress don't have the ability to argue with them They sits congress ,It were an information ploy ,to let the public no that the bucks stop here .We accept ourselves just as we are, it was I that choose to be what I am, and no one can change that , Far from the truth, you were raised in a culture that set the standard for moral issues long before you were born. We choose to believe that this is the right way ,in order to satisfy our ongoing ego ,thus someone gets hurt in the bargaining .The in crowd is in ,You lead, follow, or get step on.....no in between .We are in a ,"Simon say's," society and it's a mystery as to what will pop up next, Majority rule will stand as long as there is no pressure from the right opponent ,. and when he speak everyone listen weather he be right or wrong they will not take a vote if it's going to be a negative one , the wait and see syndrome takes over to see how close he is right ,if at all, and action has to be taken regardless of the circumstances. Slave was being accused of being inferior and a lot of states denied their rights and for one time the supreme court stood against congress,possibly knowing the were going to win anyway, They held that the thirteenth amendment did not hold true to private discrimination and that slaves should have equal protection under the law Two hundred years later you see some glimmer of that hope ,with the passing of the Civil Rights of 1968 , the court reverse it self and found that congress do have the right to prevent discrimination it was section two that were really the the tool that set African American free under false condition that they would not accept even until this day The struggle of racism is alive and well parcel freedom has been deem as no freedom at all ,The dream has been realized but the nightmare didn't go

Joseph W. Kincade Jr

away ,we scream education but would rather build a bomb to kill somebody, state test has proven that Americans have the lowest S.A.T scores in the world ,and the A.C.T is not having any parades ,! Why ,? Because we give our children a false sense of security you are protected by the laws of the United States Of America , then why are there so many 19 and 20 year old on welfare we can't pull them out of the streets to get them in school let a lone give them a good education ,teachers that have a B. S degree is not going to bring up the standards of our system the pay is no more that a garbage collector if as much ,Mr Buffet ,Ms Winfrey and Mr. Gates has money and the talent to do something about the school situation but yet they choose to by-pass the ghettos of Los Angles or Harlem Or Chicago's south side ,I say to those people that a diamond came from a coal mine withstood pressure and was perfected into a gem of quality and beauty the only resource that we have is our youth get them of the streets and get rough with the drugs dealers and demand their exit from society ,we do not apologizes for our attitude gold chains and hopped up cars do not put food on the table, and embrace our kids mistakes ,don't criticize, its worst that telling them they have to move because of their associates.

Popularity ,belong to someone or something I can talk to Johnny Drug Dealer he listen ,Mom and Pop condemns .Sitting here in this cell I have a lot of time to think, momma say take what you can and go back and get the rest later , Its a lot of criminals in here I should be able to learn something... next time I want get caught. Attitude!!,you bet.

Joseph W. Kincade Jr

Wealth At What Cost

Chapter Three

We are violent and antagonistic,yet the filter of our perfections allows us to believe that we are not,either through justification of our principals and ideals,or through blindness of our action We are envious and jealous yet we perceive those qualities as being ambition or a strong competitive drive and we are filled with greed for material goods, how we obtain them is slipping thru the crack.. In 1923 a law was written to guarantee equal rights under the law for women after the congress played with it for years it finally passed in 1972, its known as the ERA   today It has a broad scope of amendments , that cover a lot more Territory, to include women, children, blacks, Indian, and criminals but nothing about false imprisonment I really think that on both sides of the fence that the hungry to be great and heard is the driving force the ego is a terrible thing to posses if handle wrong it can cause nation to be wiped out, Hitler for example,as long as his agenda was conceived as the best way to go you were safe and his idea was that Jews was a disruptive

Joseph W. Kincade Jr

breed and need to be annihilated,falsely accusing someone of not being good as you can be devastating , it has been said that it cost the lives... of six million Jews,then to be judged by a Jew ,that might not go so well. People are sitting in prison today at a cost of millions of dollars and they are innocent ..but don't have the resources to defend themselves,.so they will sit and do hard time until some elected official say that we need to look into this a little further usually doing an election , What we fail to realize is a man posses and intellect ,will, and emotions now while you are holding him, he is building up resentment toward the system that he really want to respect and believe that it works for all people be he criminal or otherwise,the Constitution Of the United States is no respecter of person ,however the people that enforce it   might be persuade to turn a blind eye   to some degree ,it been known that some members of the court has been secretly investigated and some of their finding were not to be repeated again, yet they sit there like everything is in order ,you shouldn't be a victim of denial ,shake it off and start all over again when you quit inquiring you lose , they say a silent drum carries no sound ...thus can't be heard you know there are some lawyers that's looking for a reputation that will take a case for its merits, in other words, if he can free a man that's been falsely accused of a crime , well! His credibility score just shot thru the roof ,his service will be searched out,and his fee will be astronomical. That time with you will be well paid for. There is no better advertisement that a client .

America is a ship Called the USS America   sailing in the sea of prosperity and with its small life boats hanging high above the bow , aft and port side, forever strong, and dub the preamble and the Constitution ,which is our life boats , yet we forget they are there and go on with our own agenda not mindful of the disaster approaching   the clouds of poverty approaching, promising debt that we cant legible write the winds of change is

Joseph W. Kincade Jr

so strong telling us that we had better change our course because ruff waters is ahead,we ignore the signs and one day the ship start taking on water its a three story ship and the water has gotten on the first flour and now it s heading for the deck and once its in the captains cabin its time to get on the life boats which is the Constitution of the united States you have to lower the life boats into the water although seas are ruff , however they have withstood the test of time , Three world wars , Iraq, Iran and Vietnam protecting innocent people that has been falsely Imprisoned and some has been set free because of them ,It were knock to its knees during 9/11 but it came back standing tall and looking good its time for all Americans to get on the boats of change and ride the waves of racism hungry,homelessness, and self-serving interest learn to control that and you will find the seas much calmer and your destination assured,You first have to get on the boat of change to be effectively   together, contributions have to be from all races and change have to be synonymous with your desire for prosperity for all people not just a select few ,we have become a nation that the "we"word is rarely spoken anymore, its "I" and "My"   ,to satisfy me or not to satisfy me that is the question,i remind you of a little document that reads ,"WE THE PEOPLE IN ORDER TO FORM A MORE FERFECT UNION, I hope you remember those hallow words we have to stop all this amendment writing and stick to what the founding fathers had in mind,I am almost sure that it didn't include giving away money by the fist fulls so a country could declare war on us ,Our troops are in other countries at this writing fighting for what they was told a legitimate cause and it has been said that we go looking for a fight falsely accusing the opponents of some cause that don't even exist, What you see is not always what it is, Iraq was declared under false accusation it was proven and we are still there, for the first time in history the judges are getting told "

Joseph W. Kincade Jr

not so, sir" , the Constitution say's, and they are very uncomfortable with that , they are under investigation for things of the past and the congress is saying you guide us in the law ,and not your personal opinions ,two seats are coming up for grabs and the president will have to choose what kind of Justices he wants it will be the ones that fits his agenda he is not going to think about the Constitution and how it reads we are a party society now, we change the laws to fit our parties ego They(the republicans)admitted   they would not vote with the democrats for fear of reprisal even though the bill might be a goods one and when they go to their respective district they would take credit for the passing of the legislation thou they voted against it if it passed without them that is,some stood up and denied that they didn't vote for the stimulus money ,but when it start showing progress they got on the band wagon and took the long ride of false success ,or better yet down right lying the only time the "we" word was used when the bill came law ,we passed this law and the democrats couldn't decide what to vote on, announced one senator ,How determined can you get and at what cost .A man accused President Clinton of unfaithfulness,and yet he had illegal aliens cleaning his house paying no social security , an a wage that would starve you to death,you talking about cleaning the commode before you use the bathroom ,Our men and women that are in prison ,Falsely accused that is, their freedom depends on those very one's that are up in congress playing with the law that was introduced by them.,and not so inclined as to what the Constitution reads A man is innocent until proven guilty by a jury of his pears so say's the law ,but go to jail and see how long they will hold you on that charged. The drug dealers and your children are taking over this country and you just stand back and watch, your child know more about the child abuse law and its loop holes that you could ever know, the bible, say spare the rod and spoil the child the

Joseph W. Kincade Jr

state say, if you do we ware going to put you in jail,.your hands are made for working not spanking and I am sitting here making sure you comply,I heard a preacher stand up in the pulpit and say that low rider pants were a culture , where he came from is yet a mystery to me .

Lets face it we are in trouble,now what we are going to do about it truth is hard to swallow , If you weren't going to digest it in the first place, I know a lady that were eight five years old had two adopted children and they grew up to be outlaws ,the judge that let her had them should be locked up,adopting children after you pass your Sixty fifth birthday is asking for trouble especially if they are crack babies, they called her ma Barker .after the former lady in history , that's sad There is nothing those kids wanted that she didn't supply she was pretty well off at one time she died a pauper and those kids are teenagers now and in the drug world for survival ,that's where they will be until the inevitable come and it will come. Look don't take for granted that you are taught whats right ,there is a thing called selfish love,it doesn't matter what kind of man you turn out to be just so I raise you now People are falsely accused of a many things on a daily bases ,and the person that doing the accusing never knew how the accused were brought up,mostly don't care as long as the point is being made in there favor ,Jesus has been accused of being crucified on Friday by most of the church's in America and our children follow suite, its what they been taught ,read your bible America lets get back to the truth,if you start reading Matthews Gospel you will be on the right track,Thought I would throw that in , I am all for work ethics and pleasure and I am also for accountability regardless of the position you are holding ,when a person can spend years in the penitentiary and found innocent later on and know one is held accountable its a sad day in America. What you think in a court of law don't have much weight against the Constitution and that's

Joseph W. Kincade Jr

what every law that is written should be base on ,and I did say should,You are not in any trouble until the gavel falls,its either going to be in your favor or against you,We have come to as a society that been incarcerated dose not matter the old saying the pen was not made for animals not thinking of your pride ,or moral reputation, he will do anything attitude is the way to go,so the lawyers base everything on on the precept of the way society perceived it should be, or is anticipating that this will go over because this is the way society is,don't be fooled by sweet words and smiling faces ,there is a saying that the lawyer looks way beyond the courtroom even while a trial is going on he is taking notes for the appeal process, that's where he get to make more money if you have an appeal bond or can afford one, This is what I don't understand ,If a man shout fire in a building the most strictest form of the article on freedom of speech will not protect him ,even if its a false alarm careless concerns and inappropriate words will mostly land you in jail even if you are innocent, you have to analyze every word that precede out of your mouth because someone is listening for that break in the chain.

The President stood up to a Supreme Court Justice and he shouted !!foul, not me I am a supreme court justice, you can't criticize my action .In essence what he was saying I am above the law,you can?"t touch me ,i write and you abide,.There is no true justice when there are one man's law ,or twelve for that matter the law should be base upon the people's ideal and majority that will produce peace and tranquility not some self supporting or self indulging atmospheres, people is what it 's all about like I said at the beginning, WE The People ,You can't rule, hoard, or regulate emotions , they come with training from your youth ,you are taught to obey the law, respect the law and challenge the law, when you think your rights have been violated its just that simple,We have come to a place in our lives that the

Joseph W. Kincade Jr

only thing matters is that I prospers and be rich if at all possible who get in the way doesn't matter. They will take a chance with the lawyer to achieve their goal hoping that he will find some loop hole to get them out of what ever they are trying to achieve it right or some white washed idea that might make them a few thousand dollars.

A man that can go to jail or be accused of something that he didn't do and still stay cool and calm, my hat is of to you sir ,it's very few could sit still and say they are innocent and still maintain their dignity,its a challenge that no one should have to go through.

My country tis of the sweet land of liberty of the I sing ,"sometime liberty reside in a place or false hope you are push to the limit and when challenged you are told that it were denied you because of ,etc,etc,etc,never knowing what that etc is all about and surely not the meaning,How much is the cost of freedom and who do the paying it seems like the bill gets larger and larger no second thoughts to where we are going and we are looking at the end, but we can't see it , every road ends somewhere .but you might not like the ending,we accept things the way they are, to easily ,its none of my business attitude, if you will ,and it is your business if your tax dollars are at stake.

A man working for Six dollars an hour and finds himself in trouble and no bail money excessive bail is what ever amount the judge sets ,the eight amendment address that issue however not to the poor it only meant not to put the amount out of the reach of the rich, there are two sets of the law but not written,One is the constitution and the other is make up as we go, sound like a bitter person that's been incarcerated for a long time ,not hardly,George Washington said "that what a triumph for our enemies.....to find that we are incapable of governing ourselves"What he meant was that we sit and write laws that we

Joseph W. Kincade Jr

are comfortable with not knowing that the older the law gets ,the harder it is to prove that it works, it sit on the books for decades ,yet one day it will be challenged and they will hold up a book in court that reads law vs law and all though its never been used it will convict you .see the law doesn't change because some goof ball gets up and hold a book that say's the other case was judge by this, that's a law that they have written themselves and has nothing to do with the constitution ,it is mans way of saying you play the game my way. Its incredible how people can subdue people with words or laws that seems far fetch ,yet they do it everyday and most of the victims have no clue of whats going on,   their mistake ,by not taking the time to study the constitution and its not that hard the basic rights of freedom and most black people haven't ever heard of them some not even the constitution ,they depend on someone else to   know that puts them at a disadvantage, to depend on someone else for answers and you not knowing the basic rules of whats going on is idiotic you should always have a clue as to what is being done on your behalf,this is not a handshake generation anymore   if its not in black and white set it aside   people do not care about people anymore its called greed ,i am going to get rich or die trying ,how sad, The bible   say come let us reason together , society say as long as your reasoning is in my favor ,later on I will tell you a story about the devastation of gossip, falsely accusing a man of being some thing he is not ruined his whole attitude about his family, like I said at the beginning of this book What you see is not always how it is , a true story a man went hunting ,he and his wife ,and decided to camp out overnight,it was a beautiful day and the night was romantically subdued , after the day in the woods they decided to camp as close to the main entrance as they could without being noticed as campers she was a mulatto person and he was noticeable African American,The poacher thought she was white,in Alabama that

Joseph W. Kincade Jr

was a no,no they were found shot and killed and set a fire to cover up the crime, the crime was never solved and the poacher got away clean .There are a dozen stories just like this where people see what they want to see and in the end the facts are devastating no second thought to what they see ,all,they see is a nigger laying with a white women far from the truth.

There comes a time in everyone's life that decision have to be made and sometimes very painful,nevertheless, they have to made ,we as a people have to choose, whom we are going to be loyal to, or what we are going to be loyal to, some time the decision that you make is devastating to the well being of your career or to your social statues or to your integrity ,we all admit minor faults as we scramble for a place in society that put us a little above the rest the position that we desire is the one that looks down on the crowd that less fortunate than the rest regardless of what put them in that position, its a never ending struggle to be somebody that's well respected or rich, respect comes automatic with the later , and that's where accusation are made that's not true or sometimes manufactured completely opposite of what happen yet according to your status in the community, you can say just about anything you want and they will believe you .

You don't have to be an honest person if you have money, the money is your guideline, here is some poor sucker sitting in the courtroom about to grab twenty five years and run with it and the suit up there pleading you case the states going to pay him around two hundred dollars to prove you are innocent {"bye", I will see you in twenty five. You see the prosecuting attorney is well known for his wins and MONEY , and nine times out of ten, half of his convictions, he is not absolutely sure of , yet he won because he had the investigative power to hire whom he pleases,private investigators, the backing of the

Joseph W. Kincade Jr

victims family, she say he say, type situation Hang some body , ease the pain that's going on inside of me , not spoken out verbally but thought vicariously , its know secret that the defendants family almost always lean with the prosecution regardless of the truth just to say thank god its over,not knowing if its the right man or not ,not really caring I feel better and everybody is happy, the prosecution will stand back and bask in his victory and the pay he received other that his salary .Let me tell you about guy who wrote a Yiddish folklore short poem, his name was Leo Rosten ,He said that one such rumor-monger had told so many malicious untruths about the local rabbi that, over come by remorse,he begged the rabbi to forgive him,and said {"tell me how I can make amends, The Rabbi explained,go to the town square and there cut two pillows open wave them in the air . Then come back , The rumor-monger quickly went home and got two pillows and and a knife , hastened to the square ,cut the pillows open and waved them in the air .Then he went back to the rabbi and explained ,"i did just what you told me "he reported to the rabbi ," Good ",replied the rabbi ,.Now to realize how much harm is done buy gossip ,go back to the square and collect all the feathers.

You see we never know how much harm our speech can cause until its to late , just like the lady that was found raped she blamed somebody not knowing for sure if he was the attacker or not she didn't care blame somebody it will be alright he is a black man anyway, so it doesn't make any difference ,what I need is satisfaction knowing someone is serving time for my crime , get real people !, this society doesn't care about your feeling , just your money, touche,!! crime victims repreration is in order ,However , some states doesn't pay for false time served , you have to go private ,and sue on anything you can come up with,just to get into court and then you can go to the real issue , back door entrance ,so to speak,,you know how they do in

Joseph W. Kincade Jr

congress they present one bill to be passed with another tied to it in small print. I understand that its being debated behind closed doors that we are to pass a bill that do not require our children to attend school , I hope for the parents sake that never happen it would be total destruction, most parents can't control their kids now being around them 24/7 is not going to help, I've come to the conclusion that if we don't make some drastic changes in our government there are going to be cast on a grand scale ,look we have to adopt and change we know that nothing stays the same but the word of GOD he says I change not ,but you have to understand what you are changing, this is the very fabric of our society you are talking about not a flat tire , The people we train today will be run the show tomorrow and some are not so worthy right now ,we should be stressing education not talking about giving the parent authority to school their children themselves, there are far to many lawsuits now with parents grievances attached , now they are contemplating parents school, to fill the court room up, that's exactly whats going to happen ,Falsely Accusing the government of not schooling your kids, education is team work its start at home and end up in the class room , Baccalaureate means beginning you have earn the right to go out and learn something about life and if you are well discipline and patient you might make a good living, the competition is astounding with your competitors challenging you for position ,The laws will change so you have to change ,our children expect more than we can imagine silently , that's why we have to have weekend family talk sessions . They sometime seem to be inverted and yet they could be taking the silent approach ,saying who cares anyway I am just here to satisfy someone else, its been said that I am not going to mount to much anyway, that accusation will defiantly get you I don't care time , How can you teach your children the fundamentals of society when they are not interacting with

Joseph W. Kincade Jr

society, school is not only about ABC's its about people , culture , ethnically learning the rules of social acceptance , and there are rules ,and all ways will be, it allows you to follow your dream with the support of other people ,and not have a misconception of "i did this all by myself ",The only way to riches is thru people .Every lawmaker in congress has their own agenda and they try and get it passed everyday   they don't really care about what their constituents think , but you can't tell it because when they speak its all for you , to make you believe that what you really think counts,then the ego kicks in and you lost.

The best known case that I ever read was the case down in Louisiana,where the guy went to the penitentiary for 22 years and his defense lawyer stuck with him thru the end , for something he didn't do I might add ,she was ridicule to no end , however her husband was right there for her and the inmate was very cooperative. They finally got a judge to agree to DNA and that's where the ball started rolling in the inmates favor her husband died in the long process , unfortunately he didn't get to see the results of his wife's hard work and dedication ,Basic human rights were denied for years ,The basic rights and freedom to which all humans beings are entitle to, life and liberty ,freedom of thought and expression and equality before the law, sound simple , let me tell you that millions have died for just those few and the sad story is the state has no apologizes in there vocabulary and I understand no compensation either, how do you fit that ,?how do you compare that to logic ,a logically explanation would help, I am not saying it would go over big with the inmate ,however we could take the same approach he did ,wait and see,it cost him a family Twenty two years of employment and prosperity.

No one like to be Falsely Accused, people like to be treated

Joseph W. Kincade Jr

with respect and able to voice their on opinions, they like to be treated equally with others. Those ,whose rights have been violated, feel a strong sense of resentment and the results can be catastrophic., if they have no means to remedy the injustices,how does a man in lock down voice his opinion and expect to get it heard , so they become extremely repressive to hold down the violence within ,Article one of the declaration state that you have unequivocal rights as a human being laid down by GOD and our for fathers. Each human being should enjoy freedom from fear of recourse, however I wouldn't try that .The minute you start opposing their views you are going to get some down time, they are never wrong,you may think that you are the only one that's has ever been there I can assure you that there are along line as we speak, .   And most of the incarcerated feel that there is no hope , however there is always hope as long as there is life there is hope. It 's been written that a live dog is better than a dead lion, so as long as there is life there is hope

Looking back over some of the things that has happen to several inmates that were absolutely railroaded you would think there would be some kind of restitution, it seems awful just to snatch a man of the streets and give him some time on a charge that you are not sure of and he will be told there are no compensation in this state for being Falsely Accused of a crime. Most of the inmates do well after incarceration, a,.lot don't but the average do, we have a percentage system in this country and it shows that most are happy and satisfied to be an American .and they will tell you that it's the greatest place in the world to live ,and some would argue that point .The handling of the cases in the judicial system has become far to mismanaged to absolutely say that the inmate got a fair trial , beyond a reasonable doubt can't be reached anymore , emotions have come into play ,especially in small town America where

Joseph W. Kincade Jr

everybody know everybody and its your friend that's on trial here,or somebody that did you wrong at one time ,all this goes on without anyone suspecting a jurors thoughts and the question they ask will all ways be intelligent and withdrawn from all scrutiny.

Living in a world of racism and bigotry depicts the intelligence and personality of the community in which you live. you wouldn't dare witness against your neighbor depends on the color of his skin and his social status...

The basic rights and freedom to which all humans are entitled to,often held to include life and liberty and ,freedom of thought and expression and equality under the law are far from that I am afraid , everyone has a right to be recognized as a person under the law ,however if you are at the bottom of the social ladder you are going to get what ever they throw at you, they consider you a menace to society and deserve what the call might be ,that innocent until proving guilty stuff it makes good reading ,ask one that's been in lock down for a period of time and see what they tell you,if they are innocent why are they locked up they haven't been proving guilty beyond a shadow of a doubt ,the answer , we convicted him or her on circumstantial evidence, and that's just being in the wrong place at the wrong time.

The essential question is why are we attached to anything. Attachments are rooted in our search for continuity,Because we feel secure in our fragile construction of our everyday existence, I won again today ,how I won don't matter ,this is what I do win and life is summarized as a game. There are situations where nothing come out of a person mouth but condemnation and the damage they do exceeds the words it takes to explain. We have built walls to keep our fears and uncertainties chain to ourselves, in return boosting our ego to a magnitude of unbelief ,we live in a ivory castle ,but the

Joseph W. Kincade Jr

foundation is made of sand .We will never be free from non violence as long as there are jealousy and envy, thus the courtroom is the super bowel of your life, you have to win to beat a glorified counsel when they lose ,it damages what motivates them ,namely their ego. Keep in mind that they get paid to win, case in point, ask him to take a criminal case on contingency , then you will have the real feel of that old saying without any money there is no honey.

CHAPTER   4

Joseph W. Kincade Jr

The Coin Has Two Sides

If you go to court with a known criminal and the lawyer lose the case , the defendant will falsely accuse the lawyer of not representing him or her adequately,thus the lawyer will try and defend himself to no avail I might add the ground rules has been laid and no amount of explanation are going to change it.

There was the lady retired , plenty of resources in her retirement income level was high,saving account in the hundred of thousands and she was 67 years old, perfect , to enjoy her retirement she decided to adopt a boy and she ended up with three ,outlaws from the core, Of Course she adopted these at three and six weeks old it probably was fun at first, her sons had died a early death,one at 20 years old and one at 39 years old, the later survived Vietnam , as a helicopter pilot,but couldn't survive the streets of America .

The boys she adopted ,as the years went by ,stayed in trouble ,every time they were picked up she was standing on the court house steps with her check book , she knew what it took to make it in our system , they rob and stole and fought and she would explain they are picking on my boys and the lawyer would try and soften her anger to no avail and by the time they were 15 years old two had been arrested 23 times and according to her philosophy the lawyers had did them wrong, yet she kept on writing the, checks of bad behavior, people had gotten to wonder if she were mental disturbed ,one time they jumped her and broke her shoulder , and at the hospital she told the nurse she had slipped and fell,the nurse in the emergency room informed her that were an untrue her boy friend had been there and told the doctors what happen and that she was to old to handle those boys at her age, She informed him to tend to his

Joseph W. Kincade Jr

own business, and threw him out ,the boys had a record as long
as the state and every one around them wanted them to leave
and her also, she had adopted there life style , if they stole
something she would reward them by buying a game , let me
remind you she was 84 years old by this time and no one mess
with her boys, if you wanted to stay friends with her, she
deserted her immediate family told them that her boys was all
the family she needed , the lawyers had a field day with her and
she kept accusing them of wrong doing if you couldn't set them
free then you were in adequate, write another check and I will
see what I can do. This went on for years the neighbors had got
so they hate to see her coming, but she had a certain charm
about her that wouldn't let you feel remorseful very long, she
attended all city council meeting and were very concerned about
the community that she were destroying,she knew more about
whats going on than some of the citizen that had lived all there
life

By this time her health were failing and she had gone thru
thousands of dollars on jail fines and high price toys and the
creditors started calling and she was considering
bankruptcy,then one Saturday evening about dusk she got that
call, the one that her sisters had been telling her would happen
one day ,you can keep him out of jail but you can't keep him out
of the graveyard ,the oldest had got shot and killed on the streets
at the ripe old age of Eighteen ,and the next were on his way to
prison and she was broke and she had begun to used her people
putting on airs like she still had a lots of money.

She died and was cremated because she didn't have the
money to pay for the funeral and it had been Three years since
the oldest one got killed and she hadn't paid the funeral home
for him, a little over eight thousand dollars, until the end she
swore that the lawyers had done her wrong , and all had been

Joseph W. Kincade Jr

very lenient on advising her that she need to put them back in the system she sad she would go broke before that happen ,and so she did ,that's about the saddest story one can write nevertheless true, you see sometime the shoe is on the other foot, the authority is getting blamed even though they have done all they can do,but in our minds of reasoning we feel that they were out for the money , most are ,now days people in a professional position are not held to the highest of standard , write the rules as we go ,and see what happen, they get paid such enormous salaries for a case they can live a year on one win, and one that knows how to manipulate law w ill be rich in a short period of time , and that's when the public will start accusing him of wrong doings. Yes !!, They get accused falsely too, the butter don't spread on one side,   a smart defendant be looking for opportunities also, to claim rights violations,rights violations is the most used law that's ever written, drug dealers walk all the time because of it ,the policeman haven't been trained in the enforcement of the constitution , all should know the first fourteen articles by hard , that's where you get in trouble.

You take the immigration laws for instance , they should be in place and enforced , the immigrants accused the USA of doing them a discourtesy ,yet all they are asking is that you register as a foreign individual and if you work get a social security card ,they are not so hard to get and if you want dual citizenship apply for it ,this country say you have to learn to recite the pledge of allegiance in English whats so hard about that , guess what half the people in this country that were born here don't even know what it is ,Sometime we have to deal with necessary evils , however, it may be all you have and you make the best of what you have ,its not a let down of your ability ,its all that have been afforded you ,like eating fatback with high cholesterol ,the dangers are there ,however, you are hungry, the people of our adjoining country are hungry for a better life, they should be giving the opportunity to do so , legal and above board , they are already facing many prejudices as a people of another distinction and its going to get worse , they are being accused of taking all the jobs , hogwash!, the Americans that won't to work are working and the jobs that's are left are being filled by what ever means that are necessary ,the show must go on attitude, if you will, there are many jobs, that have been closed, because of the labor situation,the labor unions are out to break America and send all the jobs off shore , how in the world you can create raw material, send it to a foreign country and send it back to the united states as a finish product and sell it cheaper as if were made here ,call it good business judgment, I know of a company in New York sends all the components for a television to china and china send it back as a finsh product , there is no traditional America , its over ,we are being duped into believing that we are the number one producer by economic status , no country can make it without our input , I remind you to look at the label, we are a served nation , we were raised on white gloves and mint juleps , someone to answer our beck and call ,and we place powerful people in places that will self serve our interest and advancement it is intelligence that got us this far, and it will be the self will of politicians and intellect that will destroy us .Greed has become such a phenomena in this country it shows in every household , a man on the welfare system , yet in his garage is parked a Lincoln Town car,America is feeding his family while he feed his ego, and he will falsely accused America of not doing enough, he would be working !!BUT!,the foreigners has my job ,We all posse a creative imagination , and it will work for you if you put it to work , I read of this engineer who sold pizzas, not very exciting, yet it put food on the table ,so you see the system is not at all fault here sometime its the partaker ,we won't ever learn to

Joseph W. Kincade Jr

manipulate the system its all ready put in place and has been for over two hundred years .

Most false accusation are base on assumptions ,plainly assuming something that's not in fact is a part of the way the system works , case-in-point, the black race of men are accused of have the largest gentile organ ,not so in fact, so why is it assume that all black men are very large in this area, probable because some white started the myth and we took it and ran with it like we do most assumptions , it seem away to ride the wave of masculinity , stand out in a crowd and be admired by women that assume because you are black you can fill the bill of there sexual desire , here I won't be short changed and in realty you have already been short changed in your thinking , black men are not built large necessarily ,not to the degree that every one you meet is large that's ridiculous, false accusation follow you in all walks of life , and most time it stimulate trouble , it's not the pie crust that taste bad its what put into the pie that's draws attention ,you should come to the assumption that every thing that's said should be if all at possible investigated on the likelihood of it been false ,in the world we live in making false statements is a way of life, if they are going to accomplish what we are trying to achieve,we only see the glory not the destruction,the end results not the frustration getting there ,a end maybe desired only by you, and were not designed to help or promote others in there quest for truth and happiness , it has been resolved that all men are created equal , however ,not in there thinking , the bible says that as a man thinkth so is he , to prove that point , the Constitution was base on judo Christian belief , then why aren't we praying in school .We have been lead to believe that Gods present would distract our ability to learn about Einstein , Thomas Jefferson ,George Washington and Theodore Roosevelt, which decided the rules we lived by long ago, and after much Amending we

Joseph W. Kincade Jr

still don't have it   right , How can you trust GOD on your money and not trust him with you children ,with a big insignia that reads " In God We Trust" I might add , .Its almost believable that the laws are being posted to indoctrinate the coming generation in a world system that depict socialism.

Its been written that ,If my people, who are called by my name will seek my face and turn from there wicked ways,i will here from heaven and then and only then , will i heal there land ,Judo christian nation ,? not hardly ,   God said we have to seek his face, taking him out of the system is not seeking his face,Its like saying I like the strawberries but I can't stand the cool whip, when the only way that you are going to enhanced the flavor of the strawberries is accept the cool whip. A common goal in people is to have more than they need and be in control of there destiny, that's getting harder and harder to do every time you think you have it all lined up , the rules change, and you are back to square one,how many time have you heard the president say to congress , lets discuss the future of America, however ,you have heard him say and , all the congress , The American people want this done that way without your input and most times you weren't asked no poll was taking or vote declared , its I know whats best for you , so don't gripe , a man carrying his mattress on his car had been recently evicted from his home of fifteen years, the same bank that evicted him the President had gave them Five Billion dollars in stimulus money to help such people as him , just because he had lost his job to the economy and the numbers from his unemployment check didn't add up to the bankers requirement.

Is there a rule on human suffering basically no , Most bankers want you to come out to there plush office to discuss your situation and you sit there and listen while they load you up on community action dialogue which they don't know where

Joseph W. Kincade Jr

Eight Street is ,Our hands are tied , Asking you to sell the house
if you can't keep the mortgage current, when asked where am I
going to live ,His answer Don't you have some cousin that can
put you up for awhile ,Accusation of a false nature or
insinuations, changes the attitude of a society, Falsely Accusing
someone of not being able to perform up to societies expectation
when they had no control over there situation is socialism pure
and simple,you only see further by standing on the shoulders of
giants,you are where you are because of someone else. The
United States have a double standard you can go to jail for
killing an enemy, unless you are told to do so in the time of
war ,we have come to the point where all we need is someone to
blame or accuse and condemn,you will be categorize so fast you
never know what happen Trying to live by the rules is almost
impossible,they change so fast that you never knew there was a
rule. This is what I am saying where do we stop and say , this
person needs legitimate help, he is not a career welfare person
you produce the jobs and he will go to work as simple as that , if
you don't produce the jobs I'll guarantee you the bank will be
closing soon , unless they go back to the welfare source for
them. The good old US of A, No one say that you don't deserve
the help however, To whom are you loaning the money to , the
FICO system is the most corrupt system in America there are all
kind of ways to get around the system, then the consumer is
falsely accused of not paying his or her bills. It were overheard a
government employee was talking to a homeowner about his
payments and the homeowner was trying to explain that he were
expecting some funds shortly, the government employee was
telling him he needed some money today because he had two
more years to go and he was not going to lose his job. Over this
situation , the homeowner was only two months behind. He
didn't care about this man situation all he wanted to do was
make those two years for retirement and he didn't care how he

Joseph W. Kincade Jr

made them, you're out, his ego filled and the man in the office behind the desk telling him you done a good job, there is a future for you here , mistreating people and don't take nothing in consideration, they lie all time,all they want is to look good on paper ,promotion, .incentives and two extra days vacation, and go out and brag about how good the company is to work for ,All of the time he is cutting his own throat   without a mortgagee there is no need for a mortgage specialist and ` that slip will come in your pay envelope , explaining , there is no need for your specialty any more, we are hiring broker companies to sell the houses that are vacant , its called cut backs.

We see the world as we are ,not as it is, we would rather have it our way , but that's all most impossible, we have some distorted perception that every one is for us to save us from this misguide culture,when in realty we struck the match that set the woods on fire. All laws that interpreted were to better your living condition, it don't always happen that way,we have to ride the change of influential partisan, which in effect has only one goal in mind and that's to bend what ever law that suits our agenda, its no surprise that we have such trouble getting supreme court justices seated , any time you oppose a justice you are asking for big trouble,so you vote far someone that lean toward your views, thus the law changes in your favor, and the whole time this process is going on you have to make sure that your constituents under stand the platform so you feed the news media tidbits making sure not to divulge any thing that would harm the process, thus making your candidate look bad or dishonest

False accusation have no place in society , yet it happens everyday to someones gain or greed it really don't matter which, the devastation behind it is awesome,That's where blame throwing comes in, accusing someone else of a act they didn't

Joseph W. Kincade Jr

commit and you will get more listener with that kind of dialogue than you would the bible,feed my ego please during the whole conversation that's what that little voice is telling you ',man I really scored a few points with them today ,,the fake hero and his idea of logic and stumbling all over himself,never feeling anything that's right or wrong just the feeling of Adrenalin flow to satisfy his craving to be a little bit above the rest and the lie is that someone told him ,which makes it even worse, we have a built in system that crave to be believed and some time we add or take away from the truth and that should never happen , there is a song that's say "tell it like it is" . In the long run you will be better of for it,and most time there are consequences. If you think that everything you here in a court room is the truth you are way out in left field and the team has gone home, there are more lies told in the court house, than any comedy show can produce, they are looking for a conviction , how they get it most time don't matter, i told you about this lawyer went in another lawyers brief case and got physical evidence and use it against the defendant and the accused went free, that should have never happen and the judge remarked that it didn't make any difference how he got it , that's a true story ,In America we have the awesome responsibility of fighting the very thing that's suppose to protect us, Popularity , numbers and associates weight heavily in your favor if you are ever accused of a crime or act that take some proving.

Have you ever wondered what justice is ,?Justice is that none should do any mischief to another ,unless, he has first been attacked by the others wrong doings,and then I think it would be, do unto others as you would have them do unto you , and with some percipient that might not be such a great idea ,If we could just learn to love our neighbor, as our selves, I think it would be a better world , it doesn't take much effort to say i m sorry, or thank you, the lawyers have been taught from

Joseph W. Kincade Jr

childhood that the almighty dollar is the only thing that exist that he or she should be concerned about, everything else take a back seat,and action that demonstrate honesty will take on criticism. George Washington has been criticized for having slaves doing his career ,what most people don't know there were an agreement among the slaves and Mr . Washington, that they could go free any time they desired to. Most chose to stay.

I have witness the most awesome case of self control that's ever been put to the test a man locked up for a long period of time and look his accuser in the eye with seemingly no remorse , I can imagine how he felt , why be upset there is nothing I can do, with his attitude and hope is in the same system that convicted me exoneration will be slow but it will happen . Just as the slaves of Mr. Washington justice was slow but it came with a few rough edges , nevertheless, it came, what we are enjoying today was the sweat of someone else hard work, and the racism , animosity and hatred that you see is of someone else as well ,It seems that people can't live without controversy and I think that it is the number one cause of our situation that keep us going into wars that's not really our fight , you know that let me straighten this little country out attitude, two years later two hundred American are dead and they try and figure out some scientific approach to whats going on and why it happen, stupidity on a grand scale,Then the power shift began he was bad for that slot so we have to let him go I think that the man should suggest that if you keep your nose out of other people business you will find that's all's well that end well , We chain our ideas to some government idealistic forum that repeatedly haven't worked or gotten a good revue ,even from our collages ,which is suppose to be the brains of America ,if it don't work, ask Harvard and in realty Harvard can't test the heart of a country, nor the dedication of its people , Like the man said if you ride a wild horse and don't jump of- he will threw you after

Joseph W. Kincade Jr

a while,Here in America we have been riding wild horses for a long time and getting thrown often, we monitor everything from a nuclear rector in Korea to dog fight in a citizen backyard and the dog fight will get more attention.

I don't understand why it is that most critics of America thinks that Mr Obama is your ordinary run of the mill citizen ,we brought this on our selves by categorizing people,by the have and the have not's , The man quit a job making two million a year to work for four hundred thousand , If most Americans would stop criticizing and start corpora ting this would be for a better country, it seems that they can't take a vacation without someone s permission even if they pay for it , you are struggling in these economic times because the GOP put you there, falsely accusing Mr Obama of displacing hardships is a false accusation that need to be retracted ,We have a terrific sense of accusations or finger pointing when it comes to presidents , I wonder what the other four hundred dose to change the course of this country. It seems to me that everyone is watching everyone that's doing some spending they think that shouldn't be done and the spending that's being done unnecessarily is getting away clean such as Iraq , a country that's worth about twice as much as the USA, yet we give them money and they want accept checks,i really don't blame them , We have people in this country that's literally starving to death and we accused them of being lazy ,slothful and unimportant, and we are quick to recite the words "not in America ", yes, America has a homeless population that's growing everyday and we falsely accuse them of being there ,and what got them there will never be addressed .Every problem has a root just like a house has a foundation, you have to know what the foundation is made of before you can build the house , find out why he /she is on the streets and you want have to make accusation , opinions maybe ,however, they don't have to be true , your opinion is as good as the next persons they are

Joseph W. Kincade Jr

self serving and directed at one's ego ,or it will put the listener on the defensive ,trying to choose whats right or whats wrong and in realty they really don't know because after all it just and opinion ,and we have come to the realization, the one that's expressing the opinion is the key factor in weather you should believe it or not .Jealousy,hatred ,envious and ego all these play a part in the opinion that you express ,if its not criticism in a reverse form, we love to sit back and choose sides on the subject ,whatever it may be, as long as we are winning. Why is that so important ,? Check it out and you will find that it is attached to greed or verbal destruction either one benefits the ego, Close encounter of the unforgiven kind .

A man was in the hospital after open heart surgery ,with a leg infection ,the attending doctor sent for the cardiologists that were on the case, and informed him that where the vain were removed it were infected ,the cardiologists came and looked and informed the attending physician that he were on the right path for a cure , the blame shift was all most invisible the attending physician wasn't the one that were seeing after the patient in the first place ,he was just a stand in. no acceptance of responsibility is becoming the norm in our society ,and the constitution is being tested for a legit reason of why it were written ,anything that's there and do not fit the agenda of the challenger ,they will seek to amend it. The law say that an individual that cause you to be locked up on false accusation and you endured hardship ,you are initial to compensation, you want to bet, that same law locks up innocent people all the time,we are getting better ,we now discuss the matter,"come let us reason together,it looks like I am losing, so I have to do something" .

We have to learn to talk things out before they are considered offensive, because freedom of speech is guaranteed by the first amendment and congress can't change it ,the very first words

Joseph W. Kincade Jr

will uphold that. We accused the senators and representatives of not being for the country yet we are almost always asking for more we work jobs that pay Hugh salaries and still when the product go up in price we accuse the manufacturer of ripping us off, the cause of the increase in the product price was because he had to put more into the manufacturing of it ,such as, your raise in salary and the labor unions cut, the more the input,manufacturing cost ,the more the cost of the product and we sit and explain ,"he could have done something" ,you already have, done something, you ask for more money ,and layoffs are considered.

The war of economics will continue thru out time, mans greed and thirst for position will keep him struggling to obtain a plateau that's all most impossible , because man is never satisfied.

Taking in consideration that we are not willing to take a step backward to gain a foot hold as the elders use to say, we strive on seeking our positions in life that we will be satisfied and the side effects, we ignore, or the devastation that they may cause is not worthy of the ambition that has built up in side that's disguising itself as the ego or vice-verser.,Take Rosa Parks for instant, she was falsely accused of trying to incite a riot and all she was trying to do was sit down at the first seat she got to ,after cleaning houses and .sawing all day, she merely was tired, it turn out that it was the ultimate action and she weren't aware of the consequences that were to follow, literally changing a nation. The action of the police was motivated by anger ,hate and self preservation to keep a law that was in place for all the wrong reason it was the law that put them in harms way not knowing that there was a higher law that came off capitol hill ,however, it were not handed down to the people and the constitution was not taught in public school to the extended

Joseph W. Kincade Jr

reach of its black students they were in a different sector of the city and told that they would never achieve any thing , the mentality of that was the companies need labor and education was a way out of cheap labor, and the motivation was,Greed, self serving, there that word again, at what ever cost as long as I am in control mixing of the races was as bad as drinking gasoline for alcohol   that was the sacrifice that they were not ready to accept , on the other side of the coin that's not what they wanted, the blacks just wanted to be free and a end too being treated like second class citizens they bought goods and sold them they paid there taxes   as other races, yet they were falsely accused of being inferior, equality was not on Mrs. Parks mind rather relaxation was the key to her situation yet I imagine she thought "why should i give up my seat ." I paid my fare, its not fair, so I'll just sit "Good choice. . ..

False accusations ,False confession, Depression

Joseph W. Kincade Jr

Conversation with a friend

Chapter 5

There was this kid who worked hard and minded his on business , a little shy to be honest ,stayed to himself, and had a few friends ,limited though   He went to work for a company and the CEO had a reputation for being a little slight of hand ,however, he worked his way up   and finally he was the CEO 's assistant he never saw or heard any derogatory statements that he made , so he decided to ask him why people accuse him of being , basically a crook , he look at him long and silent, finally he said you know people are looking for there nitch , and how they get it isn't important. He was also a lawyer

The law and psychology are two separate disciplines , Psychology's goal is to understand behavior, the laws goal is to regulate it ,both fields make assumptions about what causes people to act the way they do ,police will coerced suspect into making false confession using tactic that have being handed down by a psychologist in there training manuals ,for instance Questioning a suspect without the benefit of a lawyer , its called "lawyering" that's against the law ,however the interrogation will sound not as if he is digging for evidence ,but rather as if he is trying to help you and in realty he is trying to get you to confess to something you didn't do, and sometimes it will last for hours. They are trying to wear you down and you will began to feel there is no hope and you just want it over with, the next step is plea bargaining,of course you do good to refuse, never accept a plea unless you are guilty, they are going to try at there best level, to get a confession out of you, they ask you question that sound innocent enough   ,however, when they make there report ,it want be innocent, it will mostly be convicting ,if they let you read it you will swear before the almighty you did not say it ,.such as they will say, they have a witness in some cases the witness don't have to show up ,and in sexual abuse cases they don't have to have evidence The you have a right to face your accuser", don't apply in this case at least that what you will be told , then you will began to feel shock and frustration ,wondering if the system works for you and your interrogator feels like you are throw away people anyway so he keep punching till he break you down if he can ,you see you just want to go ,and then you will feel guilty of being there in the first place , then your mind start rambling if I confess , I could take my chances with the jury surly they know when someone is innocent or not No,bad mistake. try and get the issue solved before you go to trial ,Jury's have a hateful attitude toward confessor, they feel you are trying to under mine there intelligence ,they are trying to eliminate the rights of the defendant   ,in a child molestation case "hearsay " is good enough it called "Outcry Witness. You have to hold on to your innocence no matter what the out come of the trial .

Theories, interferences and speculations all will become a part of your trial and the sad part is the jury just might believe the prosecutor ,that's why its so important to try and resolved the matter before trial. The advantage you have is you don't have to say nothing, the words that should be used are prove it , I was not there and you were not there so the only person that I know was there is the alleged victim,since in my situation, where it looks like I am going to be railroaded, I am going to stand on my rights .Seems like I am going a long way around to answer your questions, however ,it;s going to benefit you

. One,I have a right to face my accuser . I have right to remain

Joseph W. Kincade Jr

silent

Two,You have to prove my case beyond a reasonable doubt. Three,Where is the physical evidence .

Four , Outcry witness have to be treated as hostile witness and in some cases have to appear in court ,i will be researching this to see what case that may be.

Five, My rights have to be read to me so I can understand them.

Six, I can refuse DNA testing under the privacy law ,(if you are innocent comply)Its a fairly new law and still in the incubator they say, but its still a law and its going to pass ,its been said that 25% of today's inmates are innocent and would win if they could get a new trial the dockets are so over crowded that you will not get one ,(if you are lucky enough get one) at all for months maybe years .

In prison the accused become passive and depressed and wondering how did I get here I did nothing, but, its because you did nothing the reason you are there ,if you are innocent, there is no way an innocent person can be locked up if they are tried according to the law and the constitution. The law say ,"you are innocent ,"until you are proven guilty,Remember," Proven Guilty," that's not so easy to do where humans are involved ,errors, mistakes all are to your advantage , Keep in mind lawyers don't know all the law if they did they wouldn't have all those books that someone else printed on theory, you see so they are trying you on someone else's research which can be wrong ,then the question arise "How you know "and he'll try to explain , yeah!!, but "how you know " the book you are in come from someone's study and research,you are trying to convict me on someone else's research, that's past gone and know one can say that its true or not, or supportive of the constitution of the United States,Look you trying to get a little light to come into

Joseph W. Kincade Jr

the tunnel ,just a little bit of doubt and it will change your whole situation,you have to almost become a psychologist , read the jurors expression , such as a nod of the head up and down could mean they are agreeing with your lawyer that's good, now your lawyers job should be to hold them there and pounce on the prosecutors cross, and make sure it stays underdog.

He went on to tell him about a lot of things that had happen to him and the false accusation would always show up,there were people that could not afford a house or qualify for that matter, and he would make it right, most of time they were in the low income bracket and living in dilapidated housing , and these are same ones who started the false accusation,Once it get out there it stays out there, and no amount of retraction is going to stop it, people want to believe the worst off anyone that's doing his job and prospering , there is no set rules for you to go by and live up to someone else expectation, before the man was convicted of rape he was living his own life and doing what he thought was a good life , now he is living a different type of life that was handed down to him by someone else and he can't get an apology , if he did it, would not change his situation, as far as the community concern, he is a convicted felon and they are not going to change, and the back talking will never stop. Such as with me, it want ever stop,Let me tell you some trues,

Remember if you are man you will always be susceptible to the allegations of sexual misconduct and it always create the presumption of guilt,and your investigators has a perverse imagination, they will ask question that directly designed to mislead you in the interview and you should submit to the interview to gain information not give it ,tape the interview with a tape recorder not a digital recorder. Look for the interviewer to say things they should not say,such as,"why should she lie"?, the answer should be "i have no idea",the police officer can be charged with a crime for the interview , and he knows this "conduct unbecoming a police officer "can be frail against him ,so during the interview he has to be in charge ,He knows that the double jeopardy clause in the constitution does not apply to him, he can be drug in to court three times on the same charge ,so it's best to talk to none unless you have an attorney present ,listen to the dates and times ,that's why a recorder is so important ,you can always play it back and refresh your memory ,some time the victims will change dates on you, in order to get a conviction.

Don't just sit and give away information that will convict you let them dig for it ,they only know what someone told them ,now its there job to prove it ,and the victim could be lying,demand proof of the allegations levied against you , know what to expect they will tell you they don't have to have physical evidence ,but without physical evidence it an allegation not a crime ,you are innocent until your are proven guilty, beyond a shadow of a doubt, So you see , by me not doing what I was suppose to do cost me my reputation,i am a very rich man so I didn't need the work to survive but the heartache I felt a many,many years, I would give it all to retract my reputation and character ,Never sacrifice your integrity for your freedom of thought, nor physical emotions,if it takes going to jail to say," I am free from your conduct and allegations ,then so be it "Most of all if you are innocent ,stay with that ,regardless of the situation before you , some people are extremely ruthless and non forgiving and just because you are innocent doesn't mean that you will get a fair trial ,most of the time a fair trial means according to someone else's rule and not the constitution and the conviction of public opinion will always stay with you . That's a true story.

I wonder where depression set in? ,the questions keep coming

Joseph W. Kincade Jr

and they will be coming the rest of your life. When a married man goes to prison his thoughts are his family ,like   I say questions will start coming up , what happens to my family ,how will they live.? Who will guide them in the right directions .and what affect will this have on my kids.

Children with fathers present have a better chance in society than a one parent home and the state takes that chance away from them by not doing a through investigation of the allegation, in order to get public assistance they divorce their husband ,if not for a unbelief that's haunts them in the back of their mind,just a fragment of suspicion that the allegations levied against her husband are true.

Lets check the statistic 80% of rapists motivated with displaced anger come from fatherless homes .

71% of high school dropouts come from fatherless homes .

85% of all youth in prison come from fatherless homes.

The same state that are suppose to be up holding law and order are causing our youth to become criminals,by taking their parents without absolute knowing if he is guilty or not ,depriving children of their parents is not great police work especially if there is no proof ,This will raise the question by the children ,if he is innocent why is he in jail,?.The word false is pejorative, its used for a lack of a better term ,we like to say just something to fill your mouth with, in any case, you have to fight what you ARE dealing without concierges thought , (maybe I shouldn't do this,or   I will get myself in trouble ,)you are already in trouble, not only you are suffering, your kids are suffering ,while your wife looks for a job, who minds the children ? ,the emotional trauma they are going thru ,who address that?,the state is not going to hire you a psychologist so you need to get back in the family as quick as possible ,before your kids start

Joseph W. Kincade Jr

forming opinions ,possibly bad ones and not necessarily against the state ,a man that has been incarnated has a lot more to lose than a few years in prison ,respect for himself ,and most of all the family will look at him in a different light , the question will come and there is no answers, the holder of the answer is not talking,if he is black you did it because all of them look a like. The federal government has assigned you a race all the census taker knows is that you have very dark skin so you are obviously African American ,you could be Black Cherokee,and there are many, it wouldn't make any difference,the government is trying to categorize you .I know of a family that's Cherokee and Scotchman ,ask for there driving license it will say African American, and their genealogy will show African American,That's where the false accusation come in and they are just filling their mouths with something .You would be surprised to no at what length some people will go for notoriety ,the papers and the T.V. cameras turn them on ,The African American people have been black ,colored ,negro and a few more choice words , however, I am talking about whats on your I.D., That can be used to legally identify you with. Why is that ? ,I had a lady to tell me she was mulatto,I said O.K ,then why aren't you identified as a mulatto,(meaning mix race_)on your I.D .Card,?.

   We make mistakes in our lives when trying to create a atmosphere of honesty and trust ,there maybe times when we are misunderstood, and we are belittle with slander,false accusations and what ever that will seem to take us down a notch and its very difficult to act calmly on the policy of man .The man that was in the previous chapters obviously was a christian ,he didn't try to strike back ,didn't curse,didn't revile and didn't attack. sex cases has a monumental response to overcome, the calmer you are, the better you chances are of winning your case,you haven't done anything so whats there are to be upset about the law is

Joseph W. Kincade Jr

running its coarse and there is going to be a day of reckoning ,when all must answer to the charges and allegations levied against the accused ,how well you are prepared to received the verdict depends on you , get rid of all your negative thoughts and believe in the system because its all you have and it will work in your favor, it sometimes need a little nudging ,because the ego of the lawyer keep swelling so big and it shadows the real issue ,unfortunately cause the case to be derailed in the direction of the prosecution ,you have to watch for signs that would execute your reasonable doubt ,the jurors has a way of believing eloquent speech's and gestures by the lawyers that's maybe not in your best interest. Actually all you have going for you in a sexual abuse case is you,they are not going to believe you anyway so you have to show a lot of calm and interest in the case because you are literally fighting for your life its nothing unusually for a person to go to jail for something he didn't do ,That the way it is ask some of the inmates that's there and thought they had a good defense , hit the pavement before the trial and investigate every conceivable piece of evidence that you can find, you are not working to free your self only, but your family as well, if you do time your family will do time also.

Put the prosecution on defense by challenge all the evidence he has all the way thru the trial Fourth and fifth Amendments grounds for suppressing evidence ,sixth Amendment to confront the government witness ,objections are a tool that you should always use it confuse the juror,Capitalize on perjury by the government witness Even down to the Bill of Particulars. The constitution has been amended so much till the lawyer can't remember what it say anymore or didn't know in the first place ,even if you mention the constitution heads are going to straighten up and that puts the jurors on notice that maybe he knows what he is talking about then you have created doubt.

Joseph W. Kincade Jr

If you did the crime then you should confess and express your sorry ,its always better to get the truth out front and over with , however if you didn't do the crime you shouldn't do the time and what ever might befall you stick with your innocent don't try to beat the system it has a way of come back to haunt you ,the feeling among your accusers is, we let a guilty man walk even though you are innocent, they hate to lose and after the trial is over ,they will be looking at ways to get you back in court no matter if you are guilty or innocent , if you won, you just pecked a hole in their credibility and that's a no,no .In America we are judge by our credibility, an how many cars we drive and how big it is , unfortunately in some cases the worst people talk about you the quicker you will get picked for the chore at hand, depending on what that might be , you can over hear conversations ,get him for a lawyer they say he is the worst crook there Is, and he can buy the judge, if you have some money ,so you see the accusations don't fit one shoe, the results are what they are looking for .Your very best approach to innocent is DNA it has been improved tremendously ,and most states will honer your request don't hang all your apples on it though, the Supreme Court has come up with a ruling that's constitutional ,however they left it up to the states to employ it. It,s called Bill C 104 .250 DNA testes has been exonerated ,how many more are incarcerated that are innocent needs to be investigated ,recantation of eye witness testimony should be a consideration, police or prosecutors misconduct where there is no DNA evidence exists, They could be wrongful convicted because there were not enough evidence to over come reasonable doubt, Most prosecutors will fight for a non post DNA testing .Most of the DNA exoneration's ,include a false witness,or confession or guilty plea ,plea bargains ,the process also induce people to confess to a crime they didn't commit in order to get lighter sentence even though they didn't commit the

Joseph W. Kincade Jr

crime ,there are some innocent that   spent time on death row,how do you explain that away, the truth is there is no way you can test to clear his name ,it just not there ,Look at the domino affect the alleged was found innocent after serving time in prison ,Go back and check how many people lied or simply didn't no what they were witness to or confessing to ,these are people that you see everyday have contact with everyday and yet they are looking for something that can't be found outside of honesty Jurors will disregard evidence if the prosecutor sounds for real and believe what he is saying ,Case in Point, If a man is charged with raping a fifteen year old girl and he is identified as being five foot -eight inches tall and weights two hundred and fifty pounds and heavy built, ,however here he stands at Six foot and weight one hundred and eighty pounds and slender built ,Whats happening here is the jurors took sympathy with the Fifteen year old and the prosecutor was convincing, the truth never came out in trial ,the accused was at work at the time of the crime ,however,he was imprison for twenty nine years for not being the rapist ,what put the ball through the up rights are they are having legislation to see if they are going to compensate him , that should be a done deal , the prosecutors and all the jurors and witness should be held accountable ,clearly the man standing in the court room was not the man she described ,They will take no prisoners if the accusation involved a child , the words out of there mouth and the thoughts in there mind is "that child don't have to lie"maybe some social worker , or a parent has gotten, her so confuse that she don't know what to think,and she don't have to bring evidence to court to convict you , but according to the constitution you have a right to face the accuser , they will try and get you out of that ,but that's your shot right there,the look me in the face and tell me I did this crime attitude, its your life and no one cares more about it than you do , Take the DNA testing , the supreme court rule that a inmate has no

Joseph W. Kincade Jr

right to DNA testing ,however they left it up to the states to employ ,it if they wish ,"come on ",If its illegal in Washington its illegal in Florida, that's one of those my rule ,or no rule.

That's the reason it is so important to get all the information before the case , once you are convicted your liberties are cut from one to one ,they maybe constitutional, but not good policy according to your accusers, DNA Works ,Inmates are being set free even those who took a plea and the ones that pleaded no contest, the system failed these people and someone should be held accountable ,Failures have faces, someone is responsible for a failure, weather it be intentionally, or through a mistake or just didn't know .Just suppose a man standing on death row ,and he swear to his innocents and all they listen to is the cry of the jury wanting blood for blood now all the rules have been carried out according to the rule book the things they should have done they didn't because they didn't have to, such as exhaust every possibility of guilt beyond a reason doubt , according to the Constitution of the United States . A man that sits on death row. for Five years, knowing he is innocent ,mentally and emotionally he has already been destroyed,how can you justify that,? I don't think there is a explanation in the rule books that would stand up ,We are stepping of the deep end of the caravan without any fore thought of the danger that lies ahead , Religions that are not about America, is trying to take over this country and they have no respect for life or moral values , Columbus brought a new breed to what we know now as America to practice the religion we call Christianity without interruption , and all should serve one god ,one faith and one baptism according to the holy bible which is our guide post ,but we have gotten away from the rules by displacing GODS ideas and holy commandants and placing them in a box for later use if we happen to need them and the results is what we see today crime running rampant children with no respect for themselves or there elders, not to blame or falsely accused the children totally, the parents and this country is partially to blame, they changed our values from one of respect, to one of, if it feel good it must be right ,thus hate and manipulation and crimes that didn't have in substance rose to academics levels,we have somebody attitude, was in play and still is till this day ,its being fought thru DNA and at a surprising success rate I might add .What we see has got to be true ,that's is the most misunderstood statement in the English vocabulary..

This man every night he would go down to the lake , about a mile and an a half away , he had a beautiful truck ,retired he didn't like to fish, this went on for about six or seven years, as they hired new policeman's , there were some rookies, that just knew he was doing something wrong, and one night they just couldn't take it, they pull him over and informed him that they knew he was selling drugs and they were going to catch him one day, this man was a great christian he didn't get all rile up he ask the officer "you are sure OF that now"? The officer replied ," Yes" you leave home every morning at ,Two A.M. And you come out on the lake and sit we know you are meeting someone although we haven't seen him yet, I can't go out there its out of my jurisdiction, but the county is watching you too ,"well I hope so." the man I am meeting is the man you should be meeting if you haven't already done so , his name is Jesus Christ ,Do you know him .?We have long conversations about the daily situations and world conditions ,and he always give me answers ,There are thousand of people in the penitentiary because of people that thought they saw something and didn't, just like you, false accusation up set a whole families life, some one told you that I was selling drugs and you took it and ran with it ,The elderly man explained ,Remember ,to always believe what you do ,not what you see.

There are thousand of stories just like that, where men have

Joseph W. Kincade Jr

lost their freedom because someone thought they saw something Illegal,its an everyday occurrence ,people are being removed from society legally without any resourcefulness, or investigation just on the strength of someones word, that's not the law , as it is written, that implying who's in control, common knowledge of the constitution will save you from this kind of harassment , it don't take a Einstein to understand it , but you have to read the first fifteen articles to no your basic rights .

Time spent on improving you is time well spent .and the returns are enormous ,being able to discuss your rights with a attorney will give him a better understanding of who he has for a client,There are few dedicated attorneys now ,so you have to be very careful in your selection that is if you have money to pay him, or he is a public defender who has just got out of law school his salary is small and he know that the only way its going to get bigger is that he has to win some cases, that's to your advantage ..Money is the motivation , don't let some hot shot attorney tell you he is doing this for any other reason , When you are growing up you parents told you to be a lawyer or doctor because that's where the money was, it was a consent preaching, it wasn't because they were trying to save the country ,they were trying to assure themselves that their child would never see poverty, today that's not a very lucrative vocation unless you get the crooks off and lock up the innocent. Its been going on since the days of JESUS. He was accused of forgiving sin and he could ,yet they accuse him of blasphemy, something that is unforgivable , they new better, they took him to Pilate, he told them they wouldn't listen, "sounds familiar ,"The constitution states your case ,yet nobody listen with out a redress of the law , so they can change it to suit there purpose. Public opinion is a awful thing it clouds ones thinking and cause them to sway of coarse, Pilate knew Jesus was innocent ,yet he had to get the opinion of the crowd ,you see

Joseph W. Kincade Jr

that's where his meals were going to come from not to mention his popularity.

Today there are malpractice attorney's ,that will sue other attorneys,you have to make sure you have a case , a man that's spent fifteen years in the penitentiary has a case , or thirty nine years for that matter ,One will receive $1.750 million dollars . I wonder when the realization will come as to where he has been , and the other will get from ,Mississippi, !!squat!! ,he has to sue ,that's ridiculous .The hard part is the attorneys and judges still believe these men are guilty, they just sued with a tool that's almost in its infancy, they will almost never admit that they made a mistake , the word is "the law say "and they will ride that anyogrim to escape personality depreciation ,which can be devastating on there part ,to a lawyer there is nothing like a "win" personality or finger pointing that say "he's good "how they arrive at that conclusion is usually another story that most of us don't want to hear about most of the time it involve a lot of none trues ,they won is the word .

Most lawyers develop a sense of security just by winning, they believe I am just a cut above the rest, and that's what they strive to retain,Its been said that the only truth that come out of the courtroom is when the bailiff say," all rise" .

Money is intoxicating , to say the least, and some people have no limit to how they obtain it

One should never keep company with misery

least, He become misery himself , then he is part of

The problem . Not the solution.   J.W.Kincade

Most lawyers thrive on someone else misery , The worst the scenario the more money he'll make , He only identifies with guilt or innocent ,depending on what side of the fence he is on,A

Joseph W. Kincade Jr

man spent thirty years for something he didn't do and died thirty days after he was found innocent and released, how can you justify that to his family. And believe me the lawyer will tell you they were right ,how many have been executed that were innocent,? Who knows ,? but one day someone is going to question that very question ,we work at everything but bringing this country back into moral sanity ,who's looking over our shoulder and what their thoughts are never realizing they can't bring sanity into your thoughts you have to do that from your own perspective and diligently seek an answer with all honesty that's acceptable to all people , its been said that you can't please all the people all the time ,however, since this a majority rule society,If thy shall not steal is a law ,then the minority should live by it also with integrity and self assuring that this law was passed on by self respecting people that were for the best interest of the country and there were no self interest involved , and money was not a factor in the decision making process , we have come to a diluted process,where you mix the ingredients as you go,"A little lie here and a little truth there and if it turns out alright you are a winner",or should I say ,"digest it" , and it feels good because I won, who cares for what reason , no matter how,I received a check for that victory ,how sad ,.We have come to an all time conclusion that "I" only matters, people are suffering because of our idiotic mistakes, and not taking a stand for what they believe is right. Jesus said you are going to suffer for my sake ,but I am going to die for your sake ,(True) He is saying its not about me,it's about you , if most of the attorneys get back to that, it would be a better world , how would you like to know that someone died on death row because of a lie , that's not very thought worthy,and remember there are scapegoats, Jesus was our scapegoat , however, it was for the good ,giving his life to save many ,and innocent man sent to the gallos for the sins of the world ,but dieing to day, and innocent for money ? I

Joseph W. Kincade Jr

think not,   you have to remember that Jesus, "said,"" for this case I came into this world ,".I would exhaust all possibilities of innocent before I convict a man that I am not sure of his guilt ,living behind bars is horrible enough ,living on death row and innocent has to be devastating.

Children today are growing up into a relax society that say I will do this tomorrow ,and the parents will uphold them in anything from low riding pants to bank robbery and most know more about their rights than a lawyer,I interviewed one ,a young man that was caught up in a drug bust ,i asked what was his possibilities of going to prison , thinking that every drug dealer I knew had been let go ,he said " I first have to find out what they have by getting them to open their discovery,""then I will know how to approach there questions". If his money is big enough he will walk , and he did , you see the innocent man don't have a chance ,because he don't have any money he has to rely on the shear truth and nothing but the truth .We live in a society where the truth is rarely heard and and forgiveness is never spoken of, if you commit a crime most times you can go free, however,if you are arrested and innocent you had better come up with a good defense .The street of America has become so crowded with teenage criminals that the innocent [people have no where to walk , and none of these issues are being addressed, our society is inflamed by hoggish roll models , that could care less of what the public perceive ,just put my name in lights , for example , Jesse James is a popular role model , Al Capone is a popular roll model , you can read about these in your school history books but you want find Jesus in them , a figure that stands for right and decency is excluded in this society ,so you follow suit as they say , if you are not in trouble, then you let the laws go as there are, protesting a lawyers decision can be deadly ,he will propose that if you could have defended your self you would have, now since they appointed me , I am in charged

Joseph W. Kincade Jr

and then he will hand you a plea,if you are innocent go to jail innocent, and when you are proving innocent, take them to court , all of them including the lawyer , they can be prosecuted for wrong doing ,you want have A Picnic doing it but it can be done , go to the library and check out the book {"Lawyers that sue Lawyers"its very interesting.

I have come to the conclusion that there will be a fight it don't matter   who win or lose the idea is to get you into court so the government can charge a ridiculous price in court cost, not to mention, what the lawyer is going to get ,We should strive to be fair in all things superseding all the expectations that one one has of us knowing that the truth will inevitable come out then the accusers will look like varmints for which they are.

Driven by money and power they sit up there and ring down justice in there on form .Not caring or thinking about the truth. Sadly someone gets hurt usually the man with the less ,money,!1 now I wonder why is that ,?It don't take rocket scientist to figure that out ,We have come a long ways, and have along ways to go, hopefully with more dignity and moral respect for one another than in the past ,Its been said that there are 200 to 300 hundred inmates in prison that are innocent , if they know this then why aren't they free ,its something wrong with that picture , There were a couple of inmates that were let go after 31 years and they are trying to figure out how to compensate them for there time there is no compensation for that, these men are 55 years old now ,they have to spend most of there money on counseling ,and for what , something they didn't do in the first place ,,Look winning and justice is not the same thing, typically if you have a slick haired silver tongue attorney out to make a buck The satisfaction is in the win not in the truth its void and null if they can get you thru the trial that's all they want you see they can't take you back without new evidence , sometimes that's good

Joseph W. Kincade Jr

you might have a chance the second go round but don't bet on it because getting into the courtroom the second time is harder than the first , you need new money and if you didn't have money in the first go round …..

 well you see what I am talking about. They are going to try to keep you out of court ,and by this time you are a psychological disaster .

    The best way to stay out of jail is to don't get caught in a situation that carries time, now days its hard to avoid trouble seems like it looks for you ,sometimes even in the church, the place of rest and renewed strength have its problems, we removed God from the courthouse,so we lost integrity and moral values at that point. Nevertheless we hang on to our self images and elusive values and call them a way of life that seems fit for every one that we come in contact with and their idea or advice is far better taken than your own ,even if its about your life , in other words you don't know whats good for you ,every since the times of Adam and Eve false accusations have rose,and we place blame where it most suited to our satisfaction ,be it the truth ,or not, and sometime, we no its not the truth... we just want the satisfaction that we won, moral issues have no precedent .

    The stress of being locked up is enough to warrant the truth , and that's not so difficult the way to express it is to open your mouth and just say it, now getting someone to believe you is a another story , that's the start of a long tradition two men the judge and your lawyer then twelve people of your peers and you have a right to pick them , like that's going to help , believe me you might have some people on your jurors that actually hate you,asking them to judge fairly is next to impossible so don't get your hopes up ,like I said in the beginning try to stay out of that position, its far easier to run than to fight , be you falsely

Joseph W. Kincade Jr

accused or not the the time and money it cost to ,prove your innocent is outrageous and the scars is forever there no one is going to believe you didn't do the crime , the only words you will hear is he/she got off , and he had a good lawyer , if you go to jail then that situation changes the lawyer you had didn't do anything, he sit there and let you went to jail, forgetting there are twelve people in the juror box that could have set you free, somebody has to be the escape goat , they will choose what side when the trial is over , in this case you are going to lose whatever the out come it don't matter your integrity has been shadowed for the next ten years or longer ,you see no one is going to believe you didn't do the crime ,they will just believe you got away with it . Now you got away with a crime ,you are a hero that's the shape the world is taking , get rich or die trying,how stupid , what rich has to do with your moral character ,? We have come to the conclusion that money is our only option.

Come let us reason together ,at what time,? When ,? or where ,? you got to be kiding your option are one or none , For instance its been proven that a drug dog or any specialty dog can be given hidden cues by his handler, can you see the opportunity for the drug dealer here , he can declare that the dog was given a cue as to his search area and in realty there might not be a drug to be found , if you are driving a car or living in a house where drugs once lived the dog can sniff that out and you might be charged with a crime , you see the scent stays with the property a long time,During a test , dogs acting on the handlers cue over two hundred times ,and there were no scent present(Handlers cue is when the dog has been trained to do a certain thing such as when a scent is detected sit down or put his head on his legs or turn and go back to his car ,he will do this on a handlers cue even though there is no scent).

Joseph W. Kincade Jr

Its not about how keen the dogs nose is , its about how well the dog has been trained Test can prove that the dug can react to the handlers cues and its been proven a test were conducted in a building where there were no drugs and the handlers were told where the drugs were to be and marked the spot with construction paper when the dogs got to where the paper were they went on cue , however , it were only paper the dogs were following the handlers cue ,he were told there were drugs at that spot there were no drugs in the building period, so it weren't the keen nose of the dog, that were being accusative, it were the handler ,now who you accuse ,the dog or the handler, to get to the bottom of this question it has been suggested that the investigation be video tape whenever the dogs are used   ,that way they can catch all the handlers cues and maybe it will save someone the heartache of being falsely accused of a crime. What the researchers are saying there is a cognitive connection between the dog and the handler .Now we are into Falsely Accusing the dog of taking hidden nods ,or what ever, from the handler and the dog don't have a clue to how sensitive his nose is to smell ,Guess who will get the blame , right , the dog ,the handler say he was reacting to what he smell, which was nothing its been proven that the dog react to the handler cue,You have to be very carefully with accusations they can cause all kinds of trouble ,and you will never change the feeling of others that witness your situation ,you will have to live with the mistakes that others made as if you had made it .Every once in awhile someone will say aren't that the guy that..........I am almost sure that's him and that goes on for years, you are no better of reputation wise, as you were while you were locked up, or you don't have to be incarcerated to get the looks of guilt just someone said something about you thru gossip and it stuck , everyone believe gossip,and that, I know what I am talking about conversation goes on and on and on, .and it destroys

Joseph W. Kincade Jr

everything in its path , mainly peoples reputation , the bible say, that   thing sitting in the center of your face right below your nose,*expression are the authors* , will destroy nations. Just like hollering !!FIRE!!!in a building and there is none , the damage is already done and its not retractable peoples lives were at stake all though there were no fire they won't ever stop talking about it

He that keepth his tongue   Keepth his soul from trouble

Joseph W. Kincade Jr

The Second Amendment
Chapter 6

, Now that's a doozie ,Man has a right to bear arms, you want a bet ,When the founding fathers wrote this they didn't have no idea what they were saying.

A well regulated Militia ,being necessary to the security of a free state ,the right of the people to keep and bear arms shall not be infringed .

Bear arms that's broad statement you see arms is not only weapons that you carry around with you like those Saturday night specials you have a right to keep and bear a tank , you have a right to keep and bear a nuclear warhead and rifles of all description , according to this amendment you are allowed the same weapon of destruction as the states and to protect yourself against same. The key word here is arms they didn't specify what kinds of arms although a tank in those days were not heard of it might have been better to not specially place a noun in a document that leaves the whole document open for criticism. Walking home or riding for that matter you are caught with a pistol in your pocket ,you will be arrested for carrying a concealed weapon , yet the second amendment reads you can bear arms for your security , cut and dried ,You don't have to wait for the state to protect you ,you can do it yourself, the crooks have better weapons than the policemen right now , and it's legal . Its what they are using them for that's illegal , but carrying a weapon is not illegal , they will make you believe that you are a criminal far beyond recovery when you could be just going to a dangerous part of town , learn some of your rights if

Joseph W. Kincade Jr

at all , and there are many , false accusation will be the stepping stone for your actions, pull the gun and you will be falsely accused of terroristic threatening , that will get you ten years behind bars and no explanation is good enough your answer will be , why are you packing anyway , this is a nice town we don't tolerate this kind of behavior ,Then the Miranda rights come next , they are trying to decided if they should read the Miranda rights,They should be read to everyone that's arrested , it seems that some criminal are not subject to the Miranda law , it designed to make sure that a person Fifth Amendment rights are not violated, by imposing self incrimination by virtue of forced confession .The person can take the Fifth or he can employee the First which guarantees freedom of speech.

There are terrorists that are about to be arrested and not read there rights , the only thing wrong with that is that the law has to be for all people by the people , you can't change it just because a man is a terrorists then you are violating your own structure ,and that's not good law , There is a investigation law you can hold him for questioning as long as he has a attorney present , so many violations has accused in the justice system that half of its inmates could probably could be set free.

No one can fight your battle in the court room like you the lawyer will be there , but he is interested in the law ,and the jury is concerned about the truth , you can't depend fate for your conditions , so you have to get up and make your condition for yourself, the judge will ask you if you have anything to say in your behalf,that's your chance , there is an old saying that reads "you may not like what I say but I am going to say it anyway", And that's a law guaranteed by the Constitution Of United States Of America , that's better than Sears and Roebuck any day. Marcus Garvey , Once said :

A man is a human being ,but much,much,much more than that, a

Joseph W. Kincade Jr

man that who never say die,and never give up , and never depend on others for the things he can do for himself ,

Fight your battles in the ring of life where the most highly thought of contender is you,(author's footnote) *In a society where the laws are in place but never employed there* are no need for a lawyer , the judgment is going to be what the judge thinks and it don't have to be with in the law , Don't be so quick to think that you are going to get a fair trial,although in America that is suppose to be the order of the day , innocent until proven guilty , and we take that to be the absolute rule of law ,how far from the truth we have strayed ,The law is design to protect the innocent and sometime we fall short of that obligation , the men that has been Falsely incarcerated in this country , I salute you 99% of them were release with a shadow over there head and they respect the same law that put them away , and are using those to clear there name and acquire just compensation, fifteen years of your life for something you didn't do is a mental mind blower , I witness one being released and the first things came out of his mouth was I want to see my children , only thing his children wasn't children anymore , He had ordered know visitors while he was incarcerated , reason, he said he didn't want any one to believe that American justice was so frail , Witnesses lie they don't always tell the truth and he had found out the hard way .And said, that he was the worlds best at saying I told you so His first Amendment rights are still in place and he believe that a person should use it to the best of his ability,he said, that a sleeping dog had been awoke in him and he intend to use the law on every occasion that confronts his constitutional rights and denies the application of the same .

Imbigious assumption are ramped they are always directed at the accused , for the more confusing the trial is, more likely it is to get a conviction,Convictions improve ones social standing,

Joseph W. Kincade Jr

So they say ,i doubt that very much , since you are a lawyer it depends on what kind of lawyer you are if you are a criminal defense lawyer you will become popular quick , if you get a criminal off, that's where we are headed in the direction of the state of mind, do as you please and the constitution will protect you .

We can no longer sit by and pretend business as useable it has already gotten out of hand and we are going to have to fix it sooner or later , most likely the former, we are leaving a mess for our hairs to clean up that will never happen even in there lifetime I know that sounds far fetched , but not impossible , There ideas are different , there goals are different and most of all, think the law was written for honest people, they never think that our founding fathers might had in mind that in order to preserve freedom, that a body of people needed a guideline line to go by , so in the course of everyday activities that every action would arrive at the same conclusion according to the guidelines that has been set , the constitution don't say I the people but rather We the people , as group of people we can challenge the laws of other countries. Laws that contradicts our way of life , and tends to destroy the integrity of our system , there is an old saying that states ,I may not have much ,but it's all I have , the constitution is all we have to stand up for us, there is no other document written ,save the bible, that has withstood the test of time and is still alive and well , Convicting men and setting men free ,causing men to be falsely incarcerated and yet the victim will use that same document to free himself from a world of astrosity that they didn't ask for, but know one believe them ,Yet they will stand hands to their chest and say, " My country tis of the sweet land of liberty of the I sing land where my fathers died and land of the pilgrims pride of the I sing, America with all of her imperfection has come from occupied feeling to a freedom that man has never known , We defend the

Joseph W. Kincade Jr

criminals and protect the rights of the innocent , Only in America you can walk the streets of Los Angles with a bible in your hand and at the same time have a colt 45 stuck in your belt and be innocent of a crime , Two articles will prove this , any document based on God's word will not fail you , Scientists have been trying to prove the bible wrong for a long time, forever it seems, they haven't made it , and they wont , GOD said, before my word fail that I have sent out ,heaven and earth will pass away, (Authors Translation)What we have to learn to do is, be in harmony with our neighbor, look out for one another, report suspicious activity in your neighborhood   .Cut down on the crime and less likely you will be falsely accused of a crime.

Young people now , hang out on corners Two or Three o;clock in the morning average age fifteen years or younger they has no hope for the future, rappers and gang bangers are there life big gold chains that say "i am in"Our welfare system is straining at the seems and social security has seen its better days ,Jobs are almost impossible to get and our youth listen to all the negative talk on the media and come up with their conclusion , which is nothing .I wonder how many times that a young person in high school has set back and dreamed of the things that he would like to accomplish in his life time , or do they ever think about it, I don't think they are ever asked , Parents has a responsibility to their kids not only to take care of their physical needs but their future also,its called preparing them for life , religiously, emotionally and physically and instill hope by providing a good education, and remind them that you have never saw a Eighty year old drug dealer , their life span usually runs around Forty years old ,if they get real lucky. Yet we go around telling our kids next to nothing about the hazards of being a dealer, their life style is secluded ,its almost like being in jail and they have to constantly watch their product and money somebody is always watching them waiting for that one mistake

Joseph W. Kincade Jr

that's going to bring in the big haul , but you haven't told them about whats out there Falsely Accusing them of being something that they don't really know what its all about ,Then the, they say indictments will come up,Well, I invite you to the book of Proverbs and read what that kind of talk will get you , that's the bible in case you don't know..You will find that most of the Ten Commandments   are your articles in the Constitution .

You should here the conversation of the man that was locked up for Fifteen Years and what he lost and gained as a father, it will bring tears to you eyes ,you can't substitute love its handed down by a higher power ,the laws that are written will stand, but the people that employ them will change them as they see fit ,supposedly on your behalf ,the ballot box could change all that .Research your candidate and make sure he holds the values you cherish and are good for all people not just some one group and self interest party ,there are more groups in America that's originated for everything from rescue the the pumpkin farmers to terrorists attacks didn't mean no harm and we get suckered in by their smooth talk and fancy words like ,!!that's the man , I trust him ! Not taking in consideration that there are four or five hundred people that going to be in his decision making process, then as soon as he get elected and thing don't go as planed we jump down his throat like its his fault for the distraction , come on people that man in the white house is just a pawn he be pushed around like a chess piece , very few things he does that don't need congressional approval and they on the hill is not going to agree with him of a different party it don't matter how good the idea is they will find fault with anything except giving themselves a raise, they can't write bad checks , no matter how much its far the congressional bank will cash it , no reprimand, you try that at your bank and you will be incarcerated before the ink cool down .I think that people should be held to the same standard of living when it comes to the law , its not going to

Joseph W. Kincade Jr

happen ,influences and money will rule your destination .Its not a new thing , that old saying its been going on for over three hundred years , it wont stop for the next three hundred and beyond ,one of the most respected men in the world ,*John F. Kennedy* was accused of being a whore monger and tyrant and a whole lot more character busters but his integrity stayed intact , one of the most influential men of his day yet he took his beating , criticized for addressing the constitution as it is written and called a communist , a raciest and a few more choice words, he stood for the application of our laws as they are written and not some amendment that would change the course of its action. There is a country song that says ,"If you don't stand for something, you will fall for anything ", how true .

The constitution has been called one of the greatest documents ever written and no doubt, it is , however, it has to applied in its original form or its meaning become useless .It can only fulfill the promise, if its contents are carried out to the letter by the ones that are responsible for our legal system .The declaration Of independence say that governments are only legitimate when they represents the govern. And that Judges that interpret the Constitution for there own legal satisfaction is almost criminal .

For example : the affirmative action law was introduce into society to encourage more minorities in to the work force of there choosing , it didn't work out that way because the program decided to address education an then the strength of the law was tested ,it came up under the jurisdiction of the fourteenth Amendment which were basically wrote to free the slaves they added Chinese and Germans as a minority which makes therm eligible for the same privileges under the law ,there were a certain grade point average that you had to carry to enter into certain Universities , however , to the affirmative action student

it didn't apply. In order to change the law they said the
Affirmative Action law was written to help the plight of the
newly freed slaves   ,therefore,it found that it were
unconstitutional to have every race or gender come under the
scrutiny of the law, in which, when a law is to change
government will come under scrutiny. Laws that come under
strict scrutiny of the government are all most every time
overturned ,We The People takes on a hold new meaning when
you start excluding people that are of a different ethnicity ., I
find that the Affirmative Action program is a necessary evil , it
was design to make sure that the African American got a fair
shake in the work place , what they are doing is trying to find
some common ground for the mistake for written a law that
address the concern of one race of people , it gets back to We
The People ,which people are you talking about ,?The justices of
The United States cannot not impose their personal views on the
rest of us , however they have been doing it for years , sometime
silence speaks so loud its deafening , Clarence Thomas prove
that , the examination lead him into innocents , by him not
volunteering information every question that the examiner ask
was directed at persecution Mr. Thomas held out that he had
been falsely accused of wrong doing and that his life style came

with the job description ,such as having breakfast with his
secretary while they discuss important issues of the day .When
you pledge alligence to something ,you had better know your
constitutional rights.

        Every since the beginning of time where humans are
involved its been said that False accusation and critical
observations have dominated human thinking., the lives that it
hurts are never spoken of ,unless its in a negative tone , for some
unknown reason we tend to look at people that are successful in
there endeavors with a bad eye and if he/she have a little run in

                              Joseph W. Kincade Jr

with the law well , you are a criminal from way back there is no hope for you and the sad thing is, it satisfies their ego , not realizing that it could be that they are more ambitious than their counterparts .

The law demands truth and that's what you are suppose to tell ,but its rarely done, now they look at it , depending on who's telling it .they judge your integrity by what your past look like not by the issues at hand thats how far we have become as a nation , at what point does it establish that you are driving under the influence....DUI if you will, for the sake of argument you can not establish a point were alcohol influences your driving or thinking,that's a psychological statement that's not been proven repetitively.

A little boy and his brother was coming our of a gas station, there was a car approaching the gas pumps the bigger brother decided he would push the younger one out in front of the car ,that was moving at a snails pace the driver stop , but not in time to avoid the little boy,the car stop on the heal of his foot , he was pushed eight feet from the sidewalk to the car, the driver was falsely accused of hitting a pedestrian,that's not so , the pedestrian was pushed into the flow of traffic. Traveling at the maximum of 2 miles an hour. However, greedy eyes saw dollar signs and could not avoid the lawyers office,Money is the root of all evil and some people practice ways to receive it, no matter what..In America we have become overwhelm with greed , it doesn't matter if the pain an suffering is on someone else , we falsely accuse the insurance companies of ripping us of but we are constantly looking for ways to beat them out of there revenues, and the only way to stay in business, for all of the bogus claims is revenue, raising it to a profit level   that intimidate most patrons .

Lets talk about domestic violence ,accusation were coming

Joseph W. Kincade Jr

in that over half of the charges are false ,however the policeman are being told to listen and write it up and let them go since the legislation change the domestic violence law ,the courts declared that to many little pester case were being brought before the court at a cost that were astronautical and they went back to the old system of separation for a night, a cool of period ,if you will ,I don't no if that reflex good Judgment a person have beat the hell of out you and then a judge say take them somewhere and let them cool off .

Where do we go from here ,?if we continue the way we are, we are doom ,if we go back to the old system we are criticized for being to harsh in some cases , what happens when the child say to his mother ,"i wont to be like my dad when I grow up " ,and dad is spending fifteen years for a crime he didn't commit , explanations are hard to come buy at those moments . We have come to as place in America that the only thing matters is the results carried out in my favor . The results for false accusations are so broad that all it takes is a phone call and someone will be on the hot seat a child can get back at a parent for something he/she think is wrong , get on the phone and call the child abuse hot line and the parent will have a lot of explaining to do, the system is full of abuses that are being overlooked and a enormous rate , they figure there reputation is more important than the child truthfulness , being told the right thing and being responsible for what you say will have an affect on the outcome of your situation , you are looking at a child that has just lied and the system is protecting that lie ,however , that child is the future of this country that you will have to live by his rules in your retirement ,he didn't learn what he has learned out of books , it came from experiences that he manipulated the system while you stood and watched , and let the child abuse officials tells you if it happens again we will take him/her out of the home , now ,answer this question who is controlling whom,?you are a parent

Joseph W. Kincade Jr

that just lost all hope for a decent child to be developed in the admiration of sanity and truth and have been found guilty of disciplining your child ,making corrections in his/her that might benefit him/her as they mature in to adulthood .

My suggestion stand on the word of God , you can't control them anyway because the courts has just gave them a blank check, write in what makes you happy and don't forget to compensate yourself for your abuse. The bible say "train a children up in the way they must go " In America the courts say "you train a child the way he wants to be trained ", drop his pants down below his butt and tattoo thug on his arm for identification , He wants to be known as the man who will lift your hair,now , that's the son or daughter of the man that was put in prison on false accusations ,who raised the child it certainty wasn't the dad he was locked up, the mother tried , but she was told they would take him away from her if she tried to discipline him again , The question is did the lawyers do everything in there power to keep the Father in the home at his trial , was the investigation well researched, ninety percent of the criminals. in America come from single parent homes ,and it seems to me if that's the case   an alleged crime should be thoroughly investigated   before the court set the stage for a another criminal .

1. The man that's gets out of prison has no rights but they wont tell you that, he has to register as a criminal even though he was proven innocent, his children will never believe he didn't commit the crime he was charged with , so he lost them ,in today's society children learn by what they see, not by what they are taught ,case in point , you tell your 15 year old to use dish washing detergent in the wash and they are watching television the announcer comes on and say

Joseph W. Kincade Jr

you should use bubble bath in the wash, guess what ,bubble bath it is, what you said did not have an affect on the decision to decided what they were going to use, and the ex-con syndrome comes on , that's what they used in prison .

You have come a long way as a parent as far as supporting your family , but discipline we lost the battle ,Then your thoughts began to take over your being and good sense of judgment, the my child syndrome , I don't want them going thru what I went thru , and you were innocent in the first place .Most cases are lost in false accusation trials did you explain that to your child ,?and defamation suits are rarely won , that leaves trust , you have to prove that the statement was made with actual disregard for truth and with malice ,maybe if you had been around to train your child he would trust you and say I believe my daddy and I am going to support him and see what the out come is going to be , but with the limited investigation that was done chances are he will fall victim to the system and the state saw to it that you would not be around to discipline your child so 85% chance that he will be falling in the footsteps of his father , though his father didn't commit a crime ,he was charged with one .

WE are criminals ,If America had been truly against Anti-Military then someone like bin-Laden would have never rose to power , One man evaded a country that has the best Military system in the world for twenty five years ,, hogwash,, the time was not right for the kill and it got right when the Black man took office . So now the squabble is he didn't have to kill him another strike at the integrity of his race ,another drop in the bucket to insure a failure at reelection .

Americas soul has become poisonous and its epitaph must read Vietnam ,false accusing a country of becoming something

Joseph W. Kincade Jr

they achieved on their own after we left,President Obama was a sitting duck set up to do what every president had wash their hands off,

Presidents are remembered for something , Mr Obama will be remembered for killing Bin-Laden ,He was a drum major for the pentagon,violence ,dishonors a nation ,and with time it will destroy it accusations and false interpretation has gone in America to long .America will never be able to support its poor as long as they take part in wars that don't concern them and most of them has no substance , no lie can live forever , it has to give precedent to the truth sooner or later , you always reap what you sow , we took God out off everything that would advance this nation forward and guarantee its prosperity,even the church, has become self serving we donate for the tax deduction and most time no question are asked , we false prepare our returns and await our refunds under false pretense and think that the IRS will never catch us and in turn they think its to expensive to collect, saving the government eighty cents -while spending fifty billion to kill people that hasn't done anything to us.

If my people which are called by my name,shall humble themselves and pray,and seek my face and turn from their wicked ways ,then I will hear from Heaven ,and will forgive their sins, and will heal their land.(2nd Chronicles 7:14) NKJ.

Sounds familiar , it should God say we are walking a tight rope and I our land needs healing and he has the solutions. Locking

Joseph W. Kincade Jr

people up without full investigations ,aborting baby's that's innocent, of our lustful desire, planned parenthood that start on some street corner and the mother so young that she can't consent to anything , yet no-ones held responsible ,yet we stand up at ball games and sing the National anthem with a pride that would defy Hitler ,The dawns early light is getting dim , lets wake up America , stand up for whats right ,it took twenty five years to catch a known criminal and we knew where he was, surly we can let the innocent go free , we once stood for truth and fair dealing now that's becoming questionable. I've got a friend that say, "What's down in the well comes up in the bucket,"

We are ruining a many lives that could be saved rather than rehabilitating , rehabilitation don't work unless you have a goal in mine,If we can come up with a solution that will work before you put that father or mother in the lock up satisfying someones ego you just might make the system work ,you can't solve a solutions buy amending a law or budget for that matter look at the operating budget for the military ,yet look at the budget for the homeless ,they don't have one. We take lives where ever we can find them, WE have set the sail the way we want the ship to sail , regardless how the wind blows , the set of the sail not the Gail's that determine the way the ship goes. My suggestion we should change our Latitude and longitude and most of all our attitude .

Peoples lives are to important for the mistakes we are making –if they are really mistake, and stop the amendment process and stick with the constitutional as it is written , we change laws to suit our own agenda when the constitution clearly say that it shall not happen ,Once you lay a foundation the building has to stand on it, change the foundation and you change the building for what it were design for in the first place . One day a trumpet

Joseph W. Kincade Jr

going to sound and justice going to descend like the sound of a rushing wind and every human being is going to confess of their wrong doings and love will rescue you again for there is no condemnation in Christ JESUS   ,Just as he forgives ,we should be as a people to forgive, the criminal will not go free ,however the steps of a good man are order by the lord .We should all strive to become good law abiding citizens , Unfortunately that is not always the case , because in a trial of false accusations someone is lying and someone is telling the truth ,it reminds you of the Psalm 109 by David but not in Davids case .the man is pleading to be honored and respected for he had done no wrong and the   accusation and slander was destroying him and he is asking GOD to help him because his enemies are seeking to destroy him without a cause ,this man realize that GOD was his helper for he said vengeance is mine so he placed the burden of proof on the rightful owner , GOD said when you accused him,my child, wrongfully you accuse me for he is made in my image and I live in him, the accused didn't throw stone for stone he went to the one that new the truth ,and was willing to defend him on his behalf ,yet he asked GOD to not hurt them but make them be shamed of their action,What a act of courage ,It must have taken every ounce of strength to take a low road when every one is against you , sometimes tears flow and the heart all but stopped and thoughts are, "what have I done to deserve this"There is a feeling of emptiness and misguided trust within our self and that gives away to the criminals who most the time no the law that will get them of .

The constitution have gave away to political prowess they would rather approve the political argument than the constitutional law .We the people are going to have to demand that a trial be conducted under the laws of the constitution and not some political mandate the right to redress is being challenged in the political arena and I think its going to win

Joseph W. Kincade Jr

according to the first Amendment. New bills are being introduced without the second thought of the constitution, that has to stop there should be constitution approval before the bill is introduced .Confucius:: was accused of being morally correct, if you didn't study his work you were consider a undesirable 'however' ,no text survived that are demonstrable Authored by Confucius, so how can we come to a conclusion on his words of morality , I am afraid we can't and it happens everyday in our system of government , we never question power , for fear of some political backlash that would cause our career to go into a tail spend , Well let me tell you something the pilot of the plane of America better get hold of the control before we crash .

It seems like those that run our political system has struck a deal with the judges , Until recently the constitution hadn't been read on the floor for longer than I am old and most of the young lawmakers didn't know what it was !Oh, they had heard of it but they thought it was something to free the slaves , and then its back to business as usual , "Its protect our elected officials at all cost Attitude ".Long established laws should not be changed for some light and transient causes, than to right themselves. The heartache and pain that's beginning to show up in our system is causing havoc already and it will be on a major agenda soon, and it will be time consuming ,so the rest of the operation will suffer and the general public will suffer for the lack of knowledge that should have been never started , or should I say we should have stuck to the rules and not let greed cloud our intellectual thinking if we have any, You have the right as an elected official to protect the rights of your constituents ,and not looking for elections that would put your retirement pay overboard the job comes with sacrifice ,The man of Illinois almost wanted to fight when he was told they were going to send him home for some wrong doing ,!!!NOOOOOO!! he cried, I don't think he had done no wrong he just accepted an appointment were handed down from the man that had done wrong,which made him guilty by association ,that's a law that need to be revamped and put before a real court of justice , if no more than to test its strength, this guy saw power no doubt and it was eating him up inside to be the senator he didn't care if it were illegal he was a senator so what , which his thinking got him in a lot of trouble its not worth it they send people to jail just on a strong suspicion that's not the constitution , we as a people should strive to bring honesty and moral values to this country, our kids are daunting with the idea, of there is no hope for a future in America ,we have a standard in education that only survive third world countries,Kids are graduating that can't read,much less do calculus , and most of the dedicated teachers are so discouraged they are looking for a better vocation, the love of there life have become a problem that at there level, they can not fix it takes judicial intervention to discuss they wrongs of the system and the moderator don't know anything about the school system that's in question, we are busing children as high as thirty five miles a day to get to class because of some school closing at a expense that's overwhelming and the justification they can't explain Millions of dollars of assets are being set idle wasting away at the tax payers expense,yet they think they are having a successful application of there policies and in truth they already have fail, themselves and our children, across America children stand at the corners before its day and wait to be bused to school thirty miles away risking there lives each time they hit the corner .No lie can live forever you have to give in to the truth you harvest what you plant .

In the senate there is a chaplain that prays over the senate ,yet the future of America sits in a classroom and can't pray over the history of this country something wrong with that picture the same people that tell you not to pray uses and old law that say they can   ,yet we are all under the same

Joseph W. Kincade Jr

constitution,seems to me what qualifies a senate pastor should qualify praying in school, according to the first Amendment Congress shall pass no law regarding religion or the Establishment thereof ,,,,,,,,,,, you see we are pickers and whats right for me and you live by it ,When you are in trouble on false accusation charges, your comfort zone just went out the window ,they will work just as hard to put you in jail as if you were all ready convicted , that where a positive attitude comes in …" I am going to beat this" a whole school district were closed down because they were accused of not properly preparing the students for life. In realty the money, that were missing ,was going to be discovered and they decided to shut the school down before they were discovered in which it would give them time to explain where the money went ,Although it didn't do any good it prove there were crooks in the system, no one was ever convicted because they were high echelon ,untouchable ,if I may ,Poor Jack Horne would have been in jail so long they would have been changed his name , don't you ever believe that one system lie, as long as there are poor in America there will be two system, we have come a long way in our system there is more money to made than ever before , and you get to keep less than ever before we pretend to be well of with all our fancy house and cars and three a four immigrant hang our in the front yard mowing a yard that would take you 45 minutes to mow at tops yet we want to be seen as successful and paying less than minimum wages we just want to look good , Its been said that its not what you have its what you look like you have, false appearances are deceiving ,what you see is not always what you get .

Your life is the product and result of choices ,you always have and always had a choice, you can choose to let some false accusation bring you down or you can to look for opportunities in face of adversities and challenges, the best way to choose is to

Joseph W. Kincade Jr

choose what I can do and what I can achieve , the way you choose to see the world creates the world in which you have to live in,Slander and false accusation are inevitable they will come and you have to learn to control your emotions,its not a Saturday night picnic , the degree of the Slander determine the degree of the fight. Jesus said "come let us reason together" It want happen, and the only reasoning you are going to get is a one sided conversation in favor off the persecutor , and they will make you look like you should be put away for your attitude even .

Lets all learn and try to be more respectful , and more concerned about others need and freedoms ,and prove there side of the story and not so quick to judge and condemn we have all made mistakes that we would like to go away but it want happen by contributing to a false swearing system , This system was built on truth and values that held us to a creed that was honorable and of high integrity,we as a people could depend on it to issue fair and incorruptible judgment .

America will survive and come out ahead after all its faults and short coming, you want find another country that you would rather live in and enjoy the freedom that we enjoy and mostly take for granted . And when you are asked ,"where are you from ,?" "you say America" they listen

Joseph W. Kincade Jr

The Constitution of the United States

The Preamble

We the People *of the United States in order to form a more perfect union , establish justice, insure domestic tranquility,provide for the common   defense ,promote the general welfare ,and secure the blessing of liberty to our selves and our posterity,do ordain and establish this constitution for the United States of America.*

Article 1 Thru 7 Omitted

The Bill Of Rights

Amendment 1

Congress shall make no law respecting an establishment of religion or prohibiting the free exercise there of .or abridging the freedom of speech,or of the right of the press , or the right of the people peaceably to assemble,and to petition the government to the right to a redress of grievances .

Amendment ll

A well regulated militia,being necessary ,being to the security of a free state ,the right of the people to secure and bear arms ,shall not be infringed.

Joseph W. Kincade Jr

Amendment lll

No soldier in time of peace be quartered in any house,without the consent of the owner ,nor in time of war ,in war ,only in a manner prescribed by law.

Amendment IV

The right of the people to be secure in their persons ,houses ,papers and effects.,against unreasonable searches, and no warrants shall be issued   ,without a provable cause. ,and Supported by oath or affirmation particularly describing the place to be searched,or the persons or things to be searched .

Amendment V

No person shall be held to answer for a capitol or otherwise a infamous crime ,unless on a presentment or indictment of a grand jury,except in cases arising from land,or navel forces,or is the militia,when in actual service in time of war or public danger,nor shall any person be subject for the same offense to be twice put in jeopardy of life and limb,nor shall be compelled in any criminal case to be a witness against himself,nor be deprived of life liberty, or property,without due process,nor should private property be taken for public use without just compensation.

This is just a few that we live by on a day to day bases, and never give it a second thought as to what they mean ,we trust the authority that's been appointed or elected over us without question, there's is gospel .Most of those things in the fifth Amendment happens everyday and we never see or say a thing to correct the validity of the offense , as long as we keep silent   more people will go to prison , innocent and on some trump up charge ,and some will be executed and yet be innocent. Its not so far fetched , it has happen in the past and will happen again , the state of Florida executed Leo James and he was found innocent after the execution,Larry Griffin was found innocent after his Execution. Timothy Cole died in prison, awaiting his execution , he was found innocent .Carlos DE Luna,   all was innocent ,and there are many more ,what do you say to theses peoples family "i am sorry?" Please,!! I am almost certain that the authorities thought they were right , however, they fell down on there investigation and then tried to correct there mistake , which made it worse , The smell of success is sometime overwhelming and intoxicating   till nothing else will do except crossing the finish line first. So doing the time that we wait for answers and none shows up the time gets longer and longer ,and every one forget what really happen even the accused are not certain he told his side right ,WE pass through different phases of life and predictable outcomes ,and pass it of as the norm ,and go with the flow and end up in front of a jury that most of them don't won't to be there in the first place, the most convincing attorney is going to win , facts are consider to a slight degree of non-exsistant or never even mention, .the authorities got what they wanted , even though it might be the wrong man ,and that ends the sage of the drama of being falsely accused of a crime that the perpetrator was the victim ..You can go on and on with stories just like this one and countless inmates can identify with it ..until we create a system that create justice for all ,this story will repeat it self over and over again,Compassion is a long word that fill a space and love is a four letter word that's synonymous with hate , sadly this country is becoming less and less popular and some blame leader ship however its been said that our citizens are the one that need to

Joseph W. Kincade Jr

take in consideration that everything voted for was against the ides of GOD , anything that goes against the word of GOD or that tend to change its purpose will fail and have severe consequence, so we sit and pretend that everything is alright , let the boat float where the river runs attitude ,How many movies have you seen on the life of Billy The Kid ?, how many of JESUS ?,You see we don't consider right or wrong or justice for all .we only consider self satisfaction. That's a momentous task for some of us and nothing takes precedent of over it .

There are trials going on in America today that's trying to convict a person and send them to prison and they haven't found evidence of any wrong doing for years yet they hold the inmate for and unreasonable amount of time on the presumption that he is guilty. fifteen ,twenty years will pass and still no verdict , and then they will find some charge hold hold you or find you innocent , in the mean time it took twenty years to learn this.

Everybody suffers in the game of law there are no innocent,victims are anyone who get caught up in the system including the lawyers and take the attitude that all well that ends well , the judge will write a letter telling the lawyers that they are fine lawyers and a credit to there profession ",Hogwash!" they saw the opportunity to make a few pointers with the judge and compensation , Men and women are being locked up everyday without the benefit of and extreme investigation ,and lawyers are not held accountable, for not putting forth there best effort, its should be criminal, a man that lives on death row for twenty one years is innocent ,that in it self prove that the courts were not sure of the conviction ,"reasonable doubt," the law was not instituted, I am the law, is the attitude, .Someday when they put GOD back in the courtroom, and they will , because if they don't there will be a outbreak of crime coming from the next generation in charge , and south of the border, that will defy all

Joseph W. Kincade Jr

reasons of sanity, they remove words and statutes and ordinances , You can't take whats in a person heart , they will always praise GOD for who he is and trust in him to guide them with out a sign or swearing with there hand held up , for he say let your answer be "yea or nay", cut and dried, and if you want to argue with him be my guess for he is willing to listen to your side of the story just before he tell you how its going to be .If you don't believe that statement ask Jonah ,Joshua ,Moses or Pharaoh for that matter .

WE as a people should come together and demand if a man stay on death row more than five years he is to be set free , if you can't convict someone in five years he/she is obviously innocent there is insufficient evidence to convict them without a doubt and all these appeal are a waste of a good person time and tax payers money when they could be out promoting society and our way of life, being asset instead of a liability. WE are going to realize one day that we are the caretaker of this world and everyone is your neighbor and GOD said love your neighbor as your self ,

Mark 12: 28-34

Of course we don't care what laws he lay down, we do what feels good. We have to realize that nothing good come out of evil, even the evil has to change if they expect something good, The recipe for changing our youth is association , you stay laid back , "man I don't deal with criminals "in reality you are no better than they are suppose they were falsely accused of a crime and then were found innocent , according to society he is a criminal that were found innocent after serving time so what now ,? you walk away ,or do you try and understand his position ?.The former will be your route because you hold societies rule in your heart, all kids are criminals and there are no hope ,

Joseph W. Kincade Jr

A lesson in self worth , "what you do for others ,will be done unto you" the neighborhoods are full of energetic youngsters that are willing to learn good habits and be known as a good kid , you don't throw out the water before you wash the dishs,all it takes is someone to ask. There are so many little league parks vacant and soccer fields ,basketball and swimming pools that you wonder if there are any kids around ,and maybe that the system has got them under such strict orders they are just scared to show themselves, or the drug dealer has shown them a little respect influence with gold chains and 24 in tires sitting on a 55 Chevy and a roll that belong to the the big guy but. They don't know that ,all false actually an a illusion .no one in drugs, ever retired on social security ,they never live long enough to sign up Most street dealers been in jail seven or eight times the judge is waiting till they turn twenty one or eighteen in some cases..

I love to read the story of Dr. Ben Carson a trouble youth who came to prominence   ,as a youth he were trouble and very disturb , he open a boys head with a knife and tried to stab him in the abdomen , but the lord had other plans he threaten his mother and was a general troublemaker with no father it was do as you please attitude,   however, his mother intervened and demanded that he study harder and read more, several books a week , he graduated from collage and went to medical school ,today he is the top neurosurgeon in this country , his autobiography tells it all there is no other success story quite like it , The book Gifted Hands will be a asset to your library. He was being falsely accused of being a nobody , but he was a somebody he was GODS child and in the midst of all the accusations he turned his life around .

The people that's sitting in prison knowing they are innocent, that has got to be the most horrifying experience anyone can

Joseph W. Kincade Jr

perceive, however , you can change things , you can demand justice and fight it until it prevail,   Mr Davis fought it until the end ,he declared his innocence until he died with more than Three million people on his side that believe in him ,There should be some satisfaction from the government to his family. There is going to be a revue of his case and all executions in this country , when we get together and stop letting the system do what they want outside the law   .Emotional pain don't end with a aspirin, scars don't heal in a life time . America stands at the bedroom of homosexuals to denounce there activity while down the road they are taking a mans life that's innocent,Gods said that he would deal with the gay person   you are to deal with Government issues , and after twenty years you can't tell me and most of the world you can't find reasonable doubt, and you kill him , without knowing that he is guilty , America sees thing as a need to satisfy there own needs and desires,and little chin chee egos . Just last week a man was found innocent after spending sometime in the penitentiary , how can you say with good conscious, the system works , it don't for most people, there is a poverty issue ,it takes money for a good defense,and most victims don't have it, and if they are accused innocent ,they are victims.

Come what may, as the old saying goes we will survive and the United States of America will continue to strive with all its mistakes and denials ,Until next time America ,......*****

To be continued ….......

Joseph W. Kincade Jr

www.ingramcontent.com/pod-product-compliance
Lightning Source LLC
Chambersburg PA
CBHW051334170526
45166CB00002B/804